THE COMPLETE MUSICIAN

THE COMPLETE MUSICIAN

STUDENT WORKBOOK, VOLUME II

An Integrated Approach to Tonal
Theory, Analysis, and Listening

Second Edition

Steven G. Laitz
Eastman School of Music

New York   Oxford
OXFORD UNIVERSITY PRESS
2008

Oxford University Press, Inc., publishes works that further Oxford University's
objective of excellence in research, scholarship, and education.

Oxford   New York
Auckland Cape Town Dar es Salaam Hong Kong Karachi
Kuala Lumpur Madrid Melbourne Mexico City Nairobi
New Delhi Shanghai Taipei Toronto

With offices in
Argentina Austria Brazil Chile Czech Republic France Greece
Guatemala Hungary Italy Japan Poland Portugal Singapore
South Korea Switzerland Thailand Turkey Ukraine Vietnam

Copyright © 2003, 2008 by Oxford University Press, Inc.

Published by Oxford University Press, Inc.
198 Madison Avenue, New York, New York 10016
http://www.oup.com

Oxford is a registered trademark of Oxford University Press

ISBN 978-0-19-530110-6

Printing number: 9 8 7 6 5 4 3 2 1

Printed in the United States of America
on acid-free paper

CONTENTS

PREFACE

Workbook II contains 104 exercises that accompany Chapters 24–37 of *The Complete Musician*. Exercises are carefully gradated, ranging from basic, introductory tasks (such as identification and comparison), to more active writing exercises within a highly regulated yet musical context, to elaborate and creative compositions that present students with more creative choices. The varied activities include not only the usual writing and analytical exercises found in many textbooks (such as spelling, error detection, figured bass, melody harmonization, and roman-numeral and formal analysis), but also crucial skill-development exercises such as singing model progressions (through arpeggiation), extensive keyboard studies, improvisation, and many types of harmonic dictation (with an emphasis on the music literature, and all performed on the instruments designated by the composers).

The second edition features a new layout: exercises are structured to fit a consistent format of discrete assignments (from four to eight assignments per chapter) fitting on usually two sheets of paper (front and back) so that students can easily tear them out and hand them in. Each assignment builds on the previous assignment and contains diverse tasks, such as analysis, dictation, four-part writing (figured bass, melody harmonization, freer illustrations, etc.), and keyboard. Thus, the instructor need not deal with the perennially thorny issue of assigning a mix of exercises that are drawn from throughout a workbook chapter, or discover that the next assignments were on the back sides of previously submitted work sheets.

In addition to the integrated assignments, numerous supplementary exercises appear at the end of each workbook chapter. Workbook 2 includes one DVD of musical examples. These recordings—from solo piano to full orchestra—present the vast majority of exercises contained in the workbook, and are played by students and faculty from the Eastman School of Music. Between the two workbooks, there are a total of nearly 2,000 recorded analytical and dictation examples.

Many people have contributed to this enterprise, and I have acknowledged them in the main text, but I would like to give special recognition and thanks to the following reviewers, each of whom worked through both workbooks and made countless suggestions: Mary I. Arlin, Ithaca College, Robert Peck, Louisiana State University, and Eliyahu Tamar, Duquesne University.

THE COMPLETE MUSICIAN

CHAPTER 24

Applied Chords

Exercises for Applied Chords (Identification, Hearing, and Writing)

ASSIGNMENT 24.1

LISTENING

EXERCISE 24.1 Aural Comparison of Progressions with and without Applied Chords

DVD 1
CH 24
TRACK 1

You will hear four pairs of short progressions; the first progression of the pair is diatonic, and the second adds applied chords that embellish the first progression. Listen to the model and write out the roman numerals. Then, listen to the second example, which contains one applied chord. For each applied chord you hear, write "V" beneath the harmony and follow it with an arrow that leads to the diatonic chord that is being tonicized. For example, if the first progression you hear is I–V–I, but the second contains an applied chord between the tonic and the dominant, you would write I–V→V–I.

A. model: ___ ___ ___

        ___ ___ ___ ___

B. model: ___ ___ ___ ___

        ___ ___ ___ ___ ___

C. model: ___ ___ ___

        ___ ___ ___ ___

D. model: ___ ___ ___ ___

        ___ ___ ___ ___ ___

ANALYSIS

EXERCISE 24.2 Recognizing Applied Chords

The following examples contain up to four applied chords. The applied chords that we will focus on are V(7)/ii, V(7)/iii, V7/IV, V(7)/V, and V(7)/vi. All are possible in both major and minor keys except for V/ii in minor (remember that dissonant triads such as ii° cannot be tonicized). For each excerpt, do the following:

1. Analyze all diatonic chords with roman numerals and give a second-level analysis.
2. Circle and label each applied chord with a roman numeral.

A sample analysis has been given. Remember to use your eye and ear to pinpoint new chromatic tones and harmonies foreign to the key.

Sample analysis

DVD 1
CH 24
TRACK 2

Mozart, Trio, String Quartet in E♭ major, K. 171

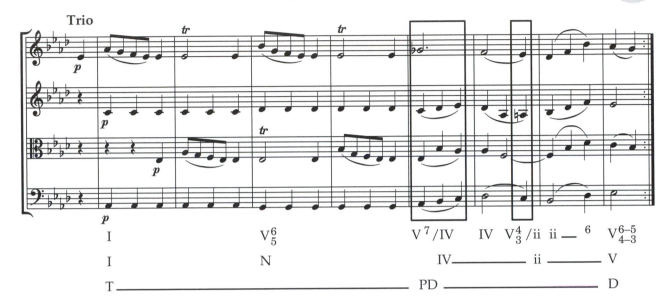

WRITING

EXERCISE 24.3 Error Detection of Applied Chords

The applied triads and seventh chords below are either incorrectly notated or incorrectly analyzed.

- For Exercises A–E: assume the *roman numeral analysis and given key to be correct*. Renotate incorrect pitches in each chord to correctly represent the roman numerals.
- Exercises F–J: *assume the notated pitches and given key to be correct*. Change incorrect roman numerals to correctly represent the pitches and given key.
- Exercises K–O: *assume both roman numerals and given key to be correct*. Renotate pitches in each incorrectly spelled applied chord and resolution to correctly represent the analysis and the given key. Correct any voice–leading errors.

A. F: V^7/IV
B. D: V^6/ii
C. a: V^7/VI
D. B♭: V^6_5/V
E. c♯: V^7/iv

F. C: V^6_5/iii
G. G: V^4_3/V
H. f: V^6_5/VI
I. f♯: V^7/III
J. A: V^6_5/V

K. G: V^7/V V
L. d: V^6/iv iv
M. E♭: V^7/iii iii
N. e: V^4_2/iv iv^6
O. F: V^6_5/ii ii

ASSIGNMENT 24.2

ANALYSIS

DVD 1
CH 24
TRACK 3

EXERCISE 24.4 Recognizing Applied Chords

The following examples contain up to four applied chords. The applied chords that we will focus on are V(7)/ii, V(7)/iii, V7/IV, V(7)/V, and V(7)/vi. All are possible in both major and minor keys except for V/iio in minor. For each excerpt do the following.

1. Analyze all diatonic chords with roman numerals and give a second-level analysis.
2. Circle and label each applied chord with a roman numeral.

A.

B. Schubert, Waltz in Bb major, *German Dances and Ecossaises,* D.783

WRITING

EXERCISE 24.5 Resolving Applied Chords

Analyze each applied chord according to the given key then lead each to its respective tonic, resolving all tendency tones correctly.

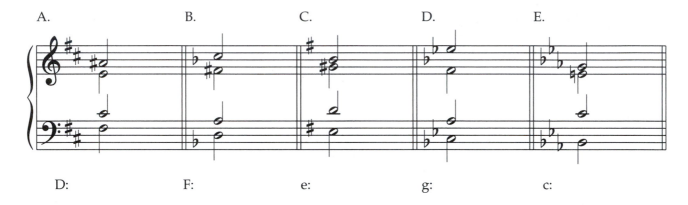

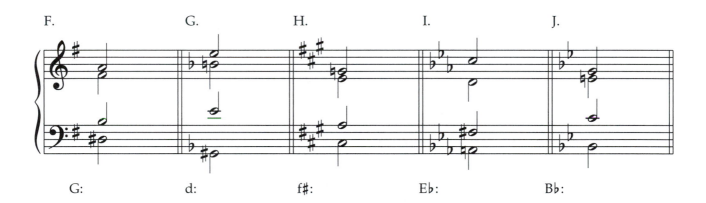

KEYBOARD

EXERCISE 24.6 Model Progressions

Play in major and minor modes as specified in keys up to and including one sharp and one flat. Be able to sing either outer voice while playing the remaining three voices. Analyze.

ASSIGNMENT 24.3

WRITING

EXERCISE 24.7 Adding Four Voices

Notate the chords as specified by the roman numerals, connecting each by using good voice leading.

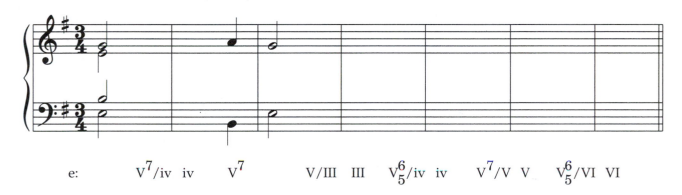

e: V^7/iv iv V^7 V/III III V^6_5/iv iv V^7/V V V^6_5/VI VI

ANALYSIS

DVD 1
CH 24
TRACK 4

EXERCISE 24.8 Applied Chords Within Phrases and Periods

Below are examples from a Beethoven trio. Provide roman numerals (use two levels of analysis), and answer any questions on a separate piece of paper.

1. In a sentence or two, discuss the phrase structure of the first passage. Is it a single phrase, a period, independent phrases, or some other structure?
2. Label the period type in the second excerpt.

Beethoven, Piano Trio no. 1 in E♭ major, op. 1, *Allegro and Adagio cantabile*

A. *Allegro*

B. *Adagio cantabile*

Note the six-four chord in m. 2. Does it function as you would expect a six-four chord to function? (Hint: Is there an underlying progression in mm. 1– 4?)

LISTENING

DVD 1
CH 24
TRACK 5

EXERCISE 24.9 Notation of Chromatic Tones

Below are notated diatonic progressions to which applied chords will be added. Notate appropriate pitches and roman numerals that reflect these added applied harmonies.

Listening tip: Remember, a chromatically raised pitch functions as the temporary leading tone to the next chord (i.e., it becomes $\hat{7}$), and a chromatically lowered pitch usually functions as the seventh of the chord that descends to the third of the following chord. The chromaticism often appears in an outer voice.

A.   B.

C. Note the parallel fifths between bass and tenor in m. 1. Added applied chords are often used as voice-leading correctives that eliminate such fifths and octaves.

KEYBOARD

EXERCISE 24.10 Brain Twister

Based on the given key signature, determine the roman numeral for each given chord in both a major key and its relative minor. Then, play and resolve each applied chord. Finally, close each example with a cadence in the major key and the relative minor key.

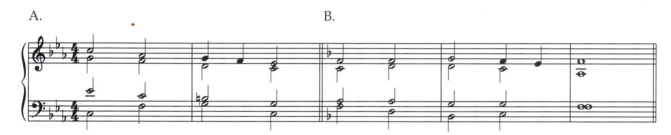

ASSIGNMENT 24.4

LISTENING

EXERCISE 24.11 Notation of Chromatic Tones

Below are notated diatonic progressions, in which applied chords will be added. Notate appropriate pitches and roman numerals that reflect these added applied harmonies.

ANALYSIS

DVD 1
CH 24
TRACK 6

EXERCISE 24.12

Provide a two-level harmonic analysis for the following examples from the literature.

A. Mozart, "Agnus Dei," Requiem, K.626

B. Mozart, String Quartet in F major, K. 158, *Allegro*

C. Elgar, "Salut d'Amour" ("Love's Greeting"), op. 12
    Make a phrase–period diagram on a separate sheet of paper.

(continues on next page)

WRITING

EXERCISE 24.13

Realize the following figured bass, which includes applied vii°6 and vii°7 chords. The soprano is given. Provide a two-level analysis.

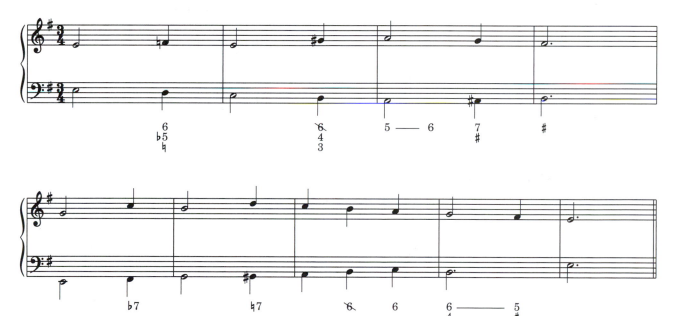

KEYBOARD

EXERCISE 24.14 Short Progressions

Add upper voices to the bass lines below. Include at least one applied chord in each example. Cast each example in a metric and rhythmic setting of your choice. Transpose to one other key of your choice.

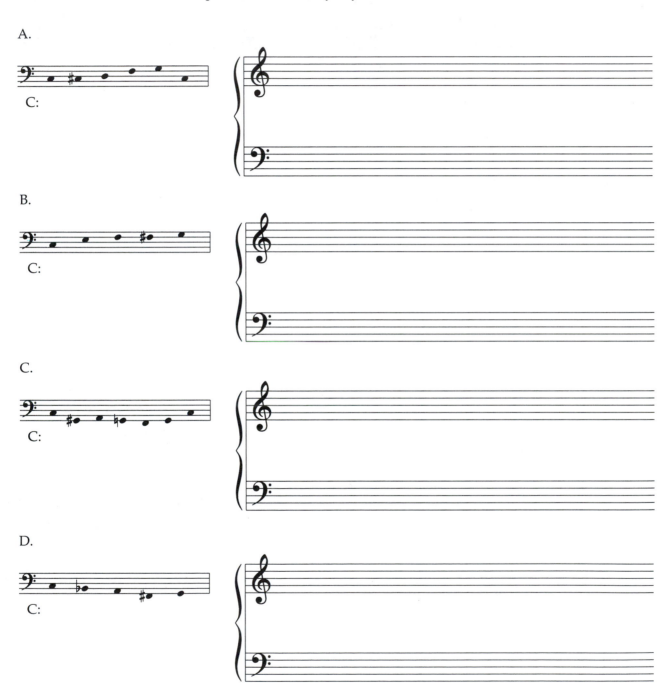

ASSIGNMENT 24.5

WRITING

EXERCISE 24.15 Applied vii°6 and vii°7

Complete the progressions below which incorporate applied vii°6 and vii°7 chords.

1. Fill in the applied chords and resolve them, then compose an ending to the progression following the instructions in each example.
2. Provide a two-level analysis.

A. After resolving the applied chord, continue using an A2 ($-3/+4$) + $_3^6$ sequence that leads to the dominant. Include two additional applied chords in this progression.

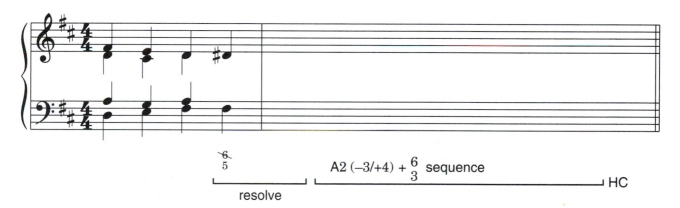

B. After resolving the applied chord, continue the progression for at least two measures, using harmonies of your choice. There must be at least two additional applied chords. Use ii$\varnothing_5^6$ as the pre-dominant. Close with an authentic cadence that includes a suspension.

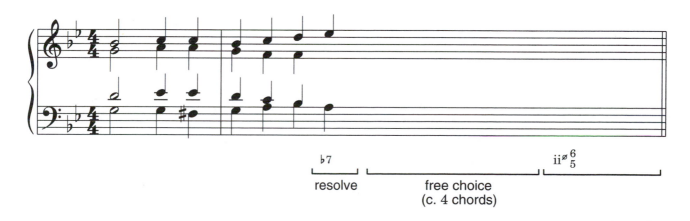

EXERCISE 24.16 Harmonizing Melodic Fragments with Applied Chords

In a logical meter and rhythmic setting of your choice, harmonize the melodic fragments by using applied chords. Arrows indicate applied-chord placement. Your harmonic progression should make sense. Analyze.

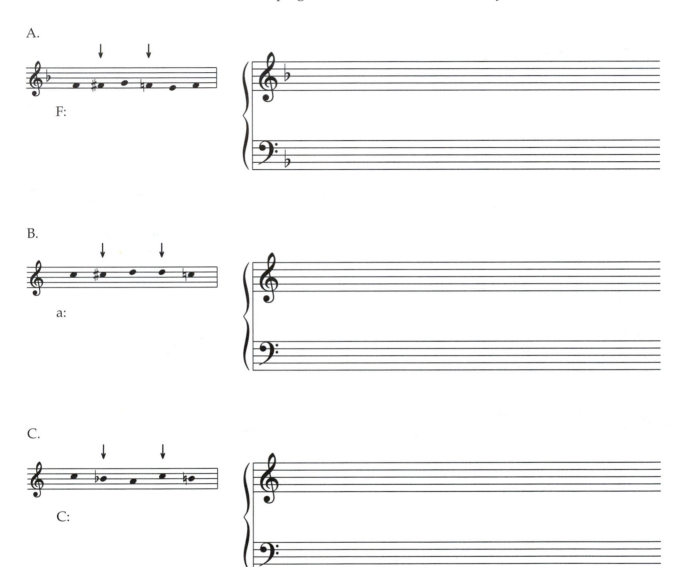

LISTENING

EXERCISE 24.17 Comparison of Applied Chords: Dominant Seventh Versus Diminished Seventh

Notate the bass and the soprano voices and provide roman numerals. Focus on whether the applied chord is a dominant seventh or a diminished seventh chord.

A.

B.

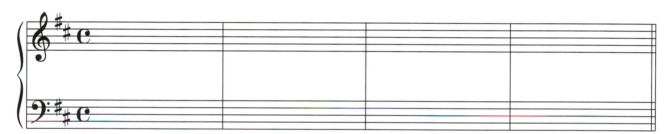

Exercises for Applied Chord Sequences

ASSIGNMENT 24.6

ANALYSIS

DVD 1
CH 24
TRACK 7

EXERCISE 24.18

Listen to and analyze each excerpt, marking the beginning and ending points of each sequence. Next, identify the sequence type by label. Finally, provide roman numerals for the remaining chords in each example.

A.

B.

C.

D.   Vivaldi, Concerto Grosso in F major, op. 9, no. 11, Ry198A, Fi 133, F.I/58, P416, *Allegro*

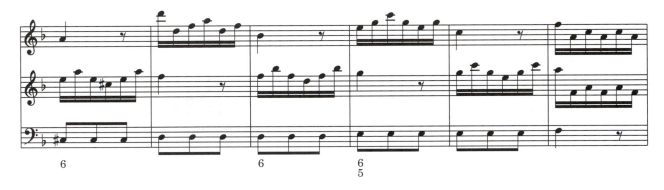

WRITING

EXERCISE 24.19 Completing Applied-Chord Sequences

Determine the type of applied-chord sequence; then continue the sequence and close with either an AC or a HC. Begin by writing the diatonic chords, and then insert the appropriate preceding applied chord.

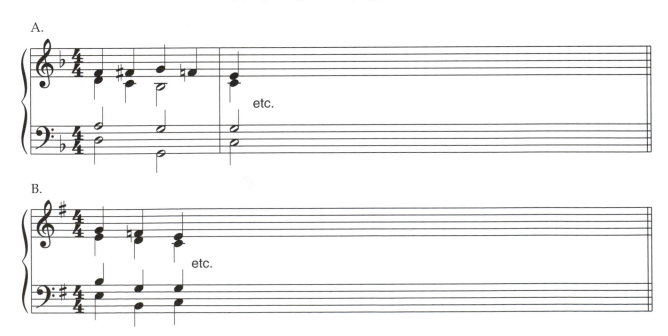

ASSIGNMENT 24.7

LISTENING AND ANALYSIS

EXERCISE 24.20 Applied Chord Sequences within the Phrase Model: Analysis and Notation.

DVD 1
CH 24
TRACK 8

The four phrases below each contain applied-chord sequences. The upper voices are provided.

1. Identify the sequence and notate the bass line.
2. Provide a two-level analysis of the excerpt.

A. Mozart, *Minuetto*, String Quartet in B♭ major ("Hunt"), K. 458

B. Schubert, Waltz in G major, *Twelve German Dances and Five Ecossaises*, no. 3, D. 529

C. Schubert, Waltz in A major, *Twelve German Dances and Five Ecossaises*, no. 12, D. 420

D. Beethoven, Violin Sonata no. 6 in A major, op. 30, no. 1, *Adagio molto expressivo*. Note that there is a slightly longer tonicization of each step within the sequence.

WRITING

EXERCISE 24.21

The figured bass below includes applied-chord sequences or sequential progressions. Add roman numerals and inner voices.

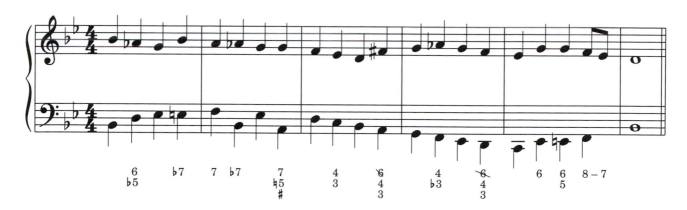

ASSIGNMENT 24.8

WRITING

EXERCISE 24.22 Harmonizing Bass Lines

Harmonize each bass line below. Each implies a diatonic or applied-chord sequence. Determine a suitable meter; you may change the note values. Analyze.

A.

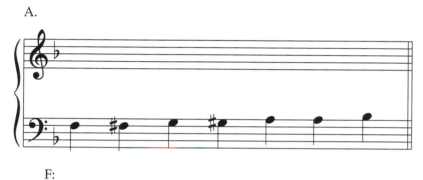

F:

B.

A:

C.

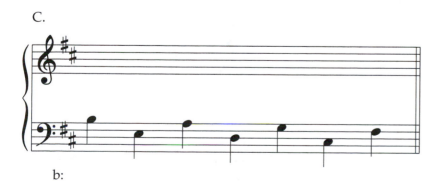

b:

(continues on next page)

D.

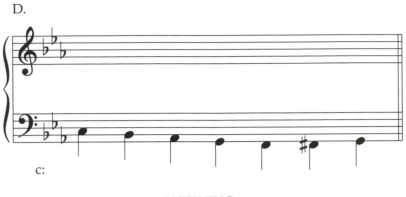

c:

LISTENING

DVD 1
CH 24
TRACK 9

EXERCISE 24.23 Notation of Applied-Chord Sequences

Add the missing bass voice by using your ear and the visual clues provided by the given upper voices. Label the sequence type.

A.

B.

C.

D.

E.

KEYBOARD

EXERCISE 24.24 Unfigured Bass

Realize the unfigured bass in four voices. Write in a two-level analysis.

ASSIGNMENT 24.9

Instrumental Application: Reduction and Elaboration

EXERCISE 24.25

Reduce the textures in the excerpts below to determine the type of sequence used. Analyze, verticalize (into a four-voice homophonic texture), and then perform each example as follows: if you are a pianist, simply play your four-voice realization; if you are a melodic instrumentalist, arpeggiate each example. Maintain good voice leading.

A. Marcello, Sonata no. 8 in A minor

B.   Corelli, Concerto Grosso in F major, op. 6, no. 6, *Allegro*

(continues on next page)

C. Corelli, Concerto Grosso in D major, op. 6, no. 4, *Vivace*

(continues on next page)

Additional Exercises

EXERCISE 24.26

Write the following applied dominant chords in four-part chorale style; write the chords in open (o) or close (c) position as indicated. Then resolve each applied dominant chord to its respective tonic. Use a key signature and add appropriate accidentals. Remember that

- Root-position applied chords can be complete or incomplete, but inverted chords should be complete.
- The temporary leading tone and the seventh of a chord should not be doubled, and they should be resolved correctly.

	Open	Close	Open
In D major:	(a) V_7/V	(b) V_5^6/IV	(c) V_6/ii
In A minor:	(d) V_7/VI	(e) V_5^6/III	f) V_2^4/V
In B minor:	(g) V_6/III	(h) V_3^4/V	(i) V_7/VI
In B♭ major:	(j) V_7/vi	(k) V_2^4/IV	(l) V_6/ii

EXERCISE 24.27

Realize the figured basses below and provide a two-level analysis.

A.

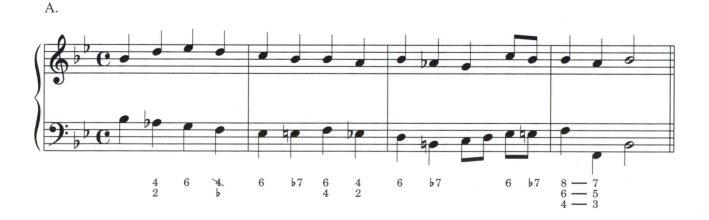

B.

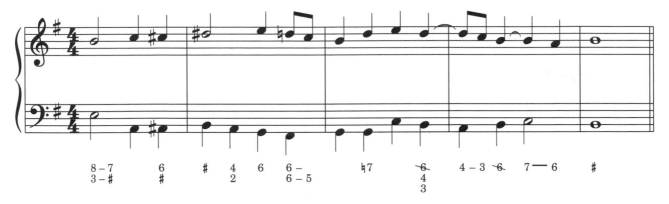

$$8 - 7 \qquad 6 \qquad \# \qquad 4 \qquad 6 \qquad 6 - \qquad \natural 7 \qquad 6 \qquad 4 - 3 \; 6 \qquad 7 — 6 \qquad \#$$
$$3 - \# \qquad \# \qquad \qquad 2 \qquad \qquad 6 - 5 \qquad \qquad 4$$
$$\qquad\qquad\qquad\qquad\qquad\qquad\qquad\qquad\qquad\qquad\qquad 3$$

EXERCISE 24.28 Applied vii°6 and vii°7

Complete the progressions below, which incorporate applied vii°6 and vii°7 chords.

1. Complete the applied chords and resolve them; then compose an ending to the progression following the instructions in each example.
2. Provide a two-level analysis.

A. After resolving the applied chords, include a descending bass arpeggiation; close with a perfect authentic cadence that includes a cadential six-four chord

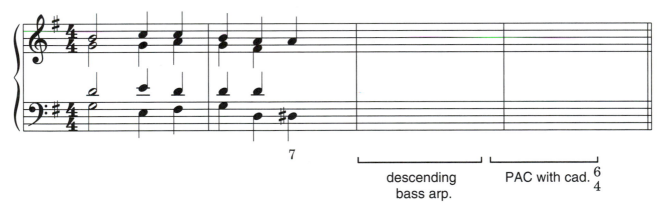

7

descending   PAC with cad. $\dfrac{6}{4}$
bass arp.

B. After resolving the applied chord, include a deceptive motion followed by ii°$^6_5$. Close with a half cadence; use an applied dominant seventh to precede the final dominant harmony.

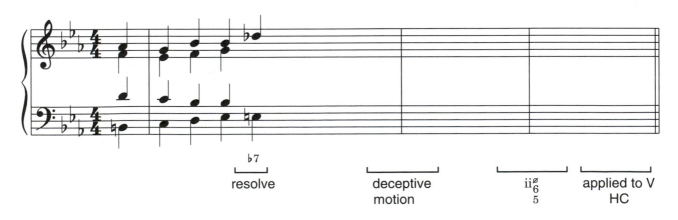

♭7

resolve   deceptive   ii$^{\varnothing}_{\substack{6\\5}}$ applied to V
                 motion   HC

EXERCISE 24.29 Figured Bass

Write a soprano line, and inner voices, and analyze by means of two levels.

A.

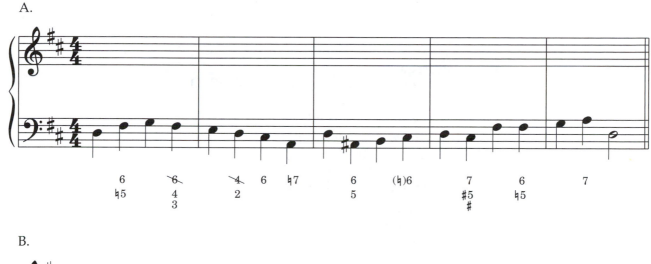

B.

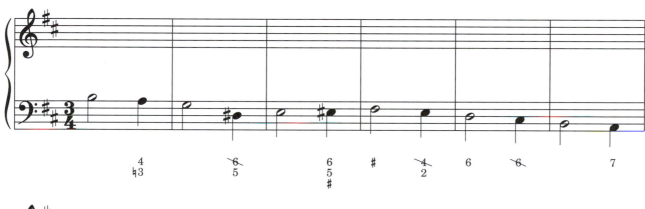

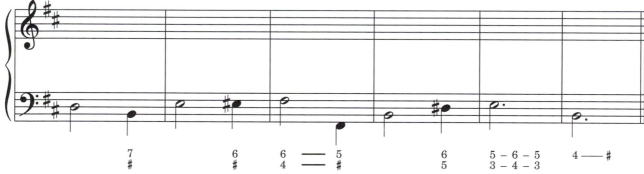

EXERCISE 24.30 Writing Phrases, Periods, and Sentences

Construct periods in four voices based on the instructions below. Analyze and label each of the required elements.

A. In G major, write an eight-measure parallel interrupted period that contains
   1. at least two applied chords in its first phrase
   2. at least two suspensions in its second phrase

      3. one example of a pedal, cadential, and passing six-four chord in one of the two phrases

B. In B minor, write an eight-measure parallel interrupted period that contains
   1. one D3 (–4/+2) sequence (may include the $\frac{6}{3}$ form)
   2. a bass suspension and at least three passing tones
   3. two examples of applied diminished seventh chords in one of the two phrases

C. In G minor, write an eight-measure parallel sectional period that contains
   1. any sequence
   2. an inverted applied dominant seventh chord
   3. a cadential six-four
   4. two accented passing tones

D. In C minor, write an eight-measure sentence that contains
   1. a step-descent bass
   2. an ascending bass arpeggiation
   3. two examples of applied diminished seventh chords

E. In E♭ major, write an eight-measure contrasting continuous period that contains
   1. an A2 (–4/+3) sequence (or its $\frac{6}{3}$ variant)
   2. a deceptive progression
   3. a suspension, accented passing tone, appoggiatura, and neighbor
   4. a descending bass arpeggiation

EXERCISE 24.31

The figured basses below (without soprano) include multiple applied-chord sequences. Write a soprano voice, analyze, and add inner voices.

1.

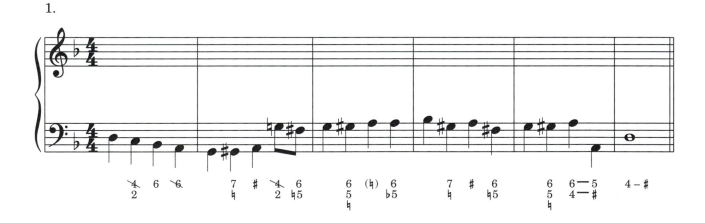

2.

EXERCISE 24.32 Illustrations

Complete the tasks below in four voices; analyze.

A. In C minor, write a D3 (–4/+2) sequence that incorporates root-position applied diminished seventh chords. Close with a perfect authentic cadence.

B. In A major, write an A2 (–3/+4) with six-threes with applied chords and an applied D2 (–5/+4) sequence (interlocking or alternating). Close with an imperfect authentic cadence.

C. In G major, write a parallel interrupted period that
   1. includes any applied chord sequence
   2. includes a deceptive progression
   3. includes two suspensions

D. In B minor, write a progression that includes the following, but not necessarily in that order:
   1. an IAC
   2. an applied chord D2 (–5/+4) sequence using dominant seventh chords
   3. a neighboring and passing six-four chord
   4. a phrygian cadence
   5. a bass suspension
   6. a tonic expansion

EXERCISE 24.33 Harmonizing Melodic Fragments with Applied Chords

In a logical meter and rhythmic setting of your choice, harmonize the melodic fragments using applied chords. Arrows indicate applied-chord placement. Your harmonic progression should make sense. Analyze.

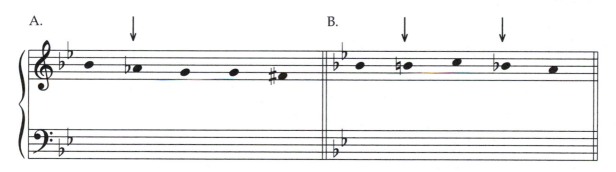

g: Bb:

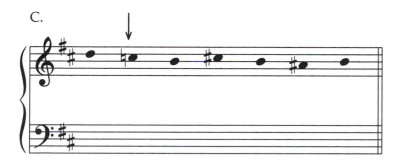

b:

CHAPTER 25

Tonicization and Modulation

Exercises for Extended Tonicization

ASSIGNMENT 25.1

ANALYSIS

EXERCISE 25.1

Below are excerpts from the literature in which a nontonic harmony is expanded through tonicization. You are to

1. listen to each phrase and bracket the expanded harmony
2. provide a chord-by-chord analysis of the harmonies within the expansion
3. analyze the remaining chords
4. provide a second-level analysis that places the tonicized area within the overall harmonic progression of the entire passage.

A.   Mendelssohn, Cello Sonata no. 1 in B♭ major, op. 45, *Allegro arioso*

(continues on next page)

B.   Corelli, Concerto Grosso, op. 6, nos. 9 and 11, *Adagio*

Below are two *Adagio* sections from two Corelli concertos. Analyze and, in a short paragraph, compare and contrast their harmonic content.

1. Excerpt B1 begins with what looks like a pedal six-four chord, but considering the chord that follows, is this the best label?
2. Consider B2 to be in G minor.

B1.

B2.

C.   Schumann, "Du bist wie eine Blume" (You Are So Like a Flower), *Myrten*, op. 25, no. 24

WRITING

EXERCISE 25.2 Figured Bass and Tonicized Areas

Study the bass for cadential patterns and the figures for chromaticism, both of which will provide a general idea of which nontonic harmonies are being tonicized. Lightly bracket each tonicized area and use a roman numeral to label it in relation to the main tonic. Then, realize the figured bass by looking for short harmonic paradigms; add a soprano, and then inner voices. Refine your initial analysis, making sure that your first-level roman numerals are consistent with the deeper-level tonicized areas.

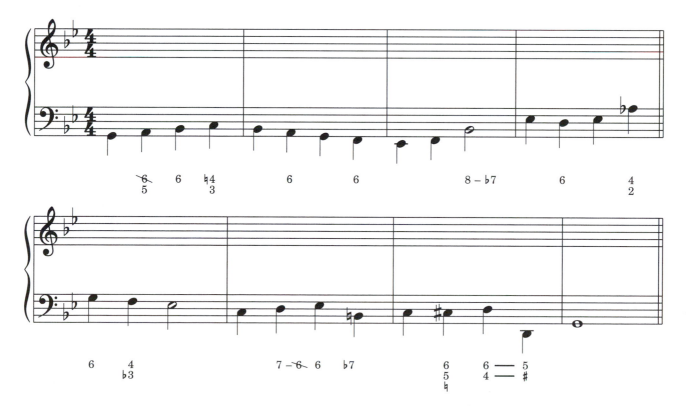

Exercises for Modulation

ASSIGNMENT 25.2

ANALYSIS

DVD 1
CH 25
TRACK 2

EXERCISE 25.3 Analysis of Tonicized Areas and Modulations

The following progressions contain either a tonicized area (in which there is a return to and cadence in the original key) or a modulation (in which closure occurs in a new key). Analyze each example with two levels of roman numerals. Use brackets to identify tonicized areas, with the roman numeral of the temporary tonal area shown below the bracket. Use pivots to show modulations.

A.

B.

WRITING

EXERCISE 25.4 Key Choices

List the closely related keys to each of the given keys. Review the various ways you can determine closely related keys.

A. D major __ __ __ __ __   B. A♭ major __ __ __ __ __   C. minor __ __ __ __ __
D. B♭ major __ __ __ __ __   E. F minor __ __ __ __ __   F. C♯ minor __ __ __ __ __

EXERCISE 25.5 Modulating Figured Basses

Realize the short figured basses below in four voices. Then analyze, being sure to label the pivot chords fully.

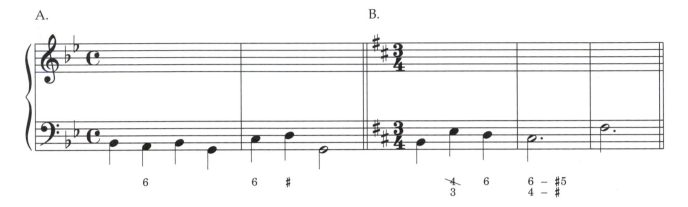

LISTENING

DVD 1
CH 25
TRACK 3

EXERCISE 25.6 Notation of Modulating Phrases and Pivot Chord Location

Each short progression modulates, closing with a PAC in a new key. Before listening, determine modulatory possibilities.

An incomplete score is given for each example. Add missing bass and soprano pitches and provide roman numerals; mark the pivot chord.

ASSIGNMENT 25.3

WRITING

EXERCISE 25.7 Modulating Figured Basses

Realize the short figured basses below in four voices. Then analyze, being sure to label the pivot chords fully.

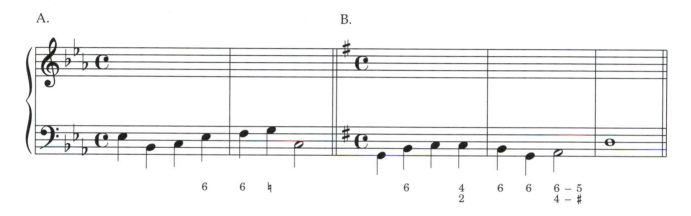

LISTENING

DVD 1
CH 25
TRACK 4

EXERCISE 25.8 Notation of Modulating Phrases and Pivot Chord Location

Each short progression modulates, closing with a PAC in the new key. Before listening, determine modulatory possibilities. An incomplete score is given for each example; the literature example is missing its entire bass line. Add missing bass and soprano pitches and provide roman numerals; mark the pivot chord.

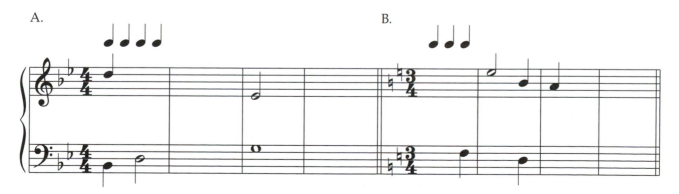

C. Haydn, String Quartet in G major, op. 64, no. 4, *Adagio*

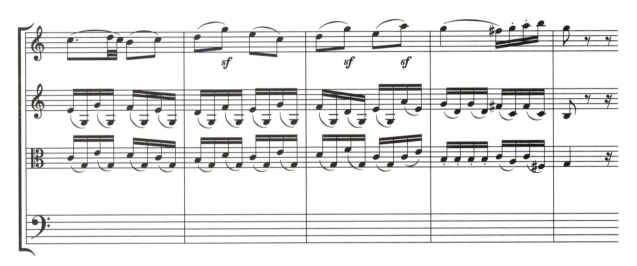

ANALYSIS

DVD 1
CH 25
TRACK 5

EXERCISE 25.9 Two-Voice Modulations

Analyze the two-phrase, two-voice modulations below. Many of the harmonies are only implied, given that only two voices ever sound together.

A.

Bb: I ———— V⁶ ———— ⁴₂ I⁶

B.

C.

KEYBOARD

EXERCISE 25.10 Multiple Tonal Destinations

Below is the opening of a phrase and its continuation, which leads to three different keys. Play each progression and analyze. Be able to transpose to one other key of your choice.

1. Use roman numerals to determine the relationship of the new key to the old key.
2. Determine the pivot chord and box it, showing its roman numeral function in the original and new keys.

ASSIGNMENT 25.4

LISTENING

EXERCISE 25.11 Notation of Modulating Phrases and Pivot Chord Location

DVD 1
CH 25
TRACK 6

Each short progression modulates, closing with a PAC. Before listening, determine modulatory possibilities. An incomplete score is given for each example; the literature example is missing its entire bass line. Add missing bass and soprano pitches and provide roman numerals; mark the pivot chord.

A.   B.

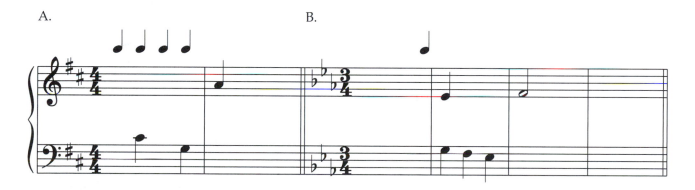

C.   Johann Jacob Bach (1682–1722), Sonata in C minor for Oboe and Continuo

(continues on next page)

ANALYSIS

DVD 1
CH 25
TRACK 7

EXERCISE 25.12 Two-Voice Modulations

Analyze the two-phrase, two-voice modulations below.

A.

B.

C.

WRITING

EXERCISE 25.13 Modulating Figured Basses

Realize the short figured basses below in four voices. Then analyze, being sure to label the pivot chords fully.

A.

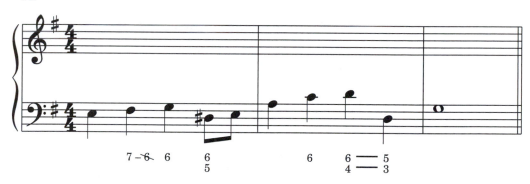

B.

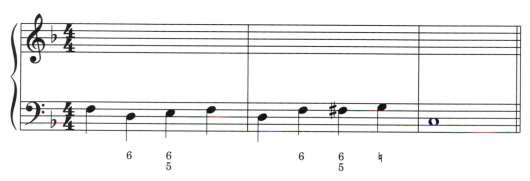

KEYBOARD

EXERCISE 25.14 Modulating Sopranos

Determine the implied initial key and the new key of each soprano fragment. Accidentals will narrow your choices considerably, but since a diatonic melody may modulate without accidentals, there may be more than one harmonic interpretation. Write out the bass line of the cadence and the preceding pre-dominant. Determine a possible bass for the opening of the progression. You will most likely end up in the approximate middle of the fragment, and the one or two unharmonized soprano pitches will be your modulatory pivot. Analyze and add inner voices.

A.   B.

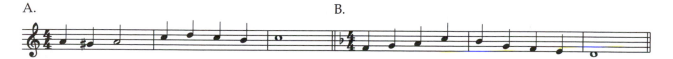

ASSIGNMENT 25.5

LISTENING

DVD 1
CH 25
TRACK 8

EXERCISE 25.15 Dictation of Longer Modulating Phrases

Notate bass and soprano for Exercises A–C and bass only for Exercises D–E. Provide a roman numeral analysis and label the pivot chord.

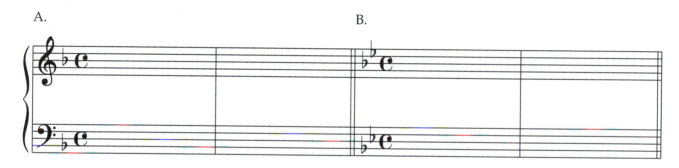

C.

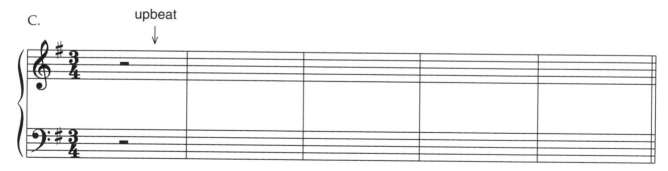

D.   Handel, Concerto Grosso in C minor, op. 6, no. 8, HWV 326, *Allegro*

E.   Mozart, "In diesen heil'gen Hallen," *Die Zauberflöte (The Magic Flute)*, K. 620 act II, scene 3

WRITING

EXERCISE 25.16   Modulating Figured Basses

Realize the short figured basses below in four voices. Then analyze, being sure to label the pivot chords fully.

A.

B.

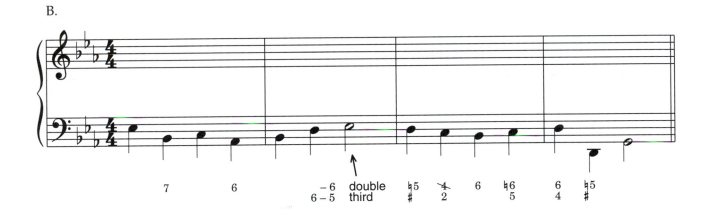

KEYBOARD

EXERCISE 25.17 Improvising Modulating Consequents

You will now work out a modulating consequent that continues musical ideas presented in the antecedent. The result will be a parallel progressive period. Study each of the three antecedent phrases and choose one. Then, begin the consequent in the same way that the antecedent began, but insert a pivot chord approximately halfway through the consequent and cadence in the new key.

A.   Zumsteeg, "Nachruf" ("Farewell"), Op. 6, no. 6

B.   Mozart, "Sehnsucht nach dem Frühlinge" (Longing for Spring), K.596

C.   Clara Schumann, "Cavatina," *Variations de Concert sur la Cavatine du "Pirate" di Bellini,* op. 8

ASSIGNMENT 25.6

LISTENING

DVD 1
CH 25
TRACK 9

EXERCISE 25.18 Dictation of Longer Modulating Phrases

Notate bass and provide a roman numeral analysis. Label the pivot chord.

A.   Haydn, String Quartet in C major, op. 54, no. 2, Hob. III: 58, *Adagio*

B.   Schubert, Waltz in B minor, *38 Waltzes, Ländler, and Ecossaises*, D. 145

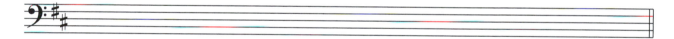

C.   Beethoven, *Lustig-Traurig*, WoO 54

D.   Haydn, String Quartet in F major, op. 74, no. 2, Hob. III: 70, *Allegro*

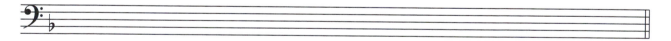

E.   Chopin, Mazurka in A minor, op. 7, no. 2, BI 61

F.   Haydn, *Trio*, Piano Sonata in C major, Hob. XVI: 10

WRITING

EXERCISE 25.19 Figured Bass

Add upper voices to the figured bass below, which modulates by sequence.

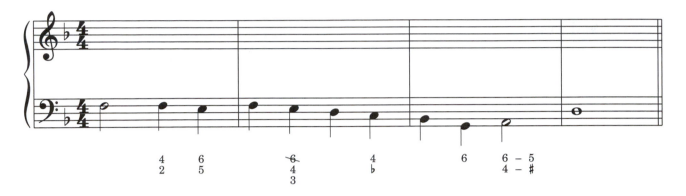

EXERCISE 25.20 Composition

A. Analyze the antecedent phrase below using roman numerals and figured bass; label tones of figuration. Then, on a separate sheet of manuscript paper, write three different consequent phrases to the antecedent, creating the following three period types: PIP, CIP and PPP (you may close in either v or III).

B. Analyze the chord progression in the first four measures of the example below. This will become the accompaniment for a melody that you will write. Then, in four voices, realize the figured bass that concludes the first phrase. Write a second phrase that modulates to and closes in a new key of your choice. Finally, write a suitable melody for both phrases.

Additional Exercises

ANALYSIS

DVD 1
CH 25
TRACK 10

EXERCISE 25.21

Below are excerpts from the literature in which a nontonic harmony is expanded through tonicization. You are to

1. listen to each phrase and bracket the expanded harmony
2. provide a chord-by-chord analysis of the harmonies within the expansion
3. provide a second-level analysis that places the tonicized area within the over-all harmonic progression of the entire passage

A.   Schumann, "Talismane," *Myrten*, op. 25, no. 8

B.   Schumann, Piano Trio in D major, op. 63, *Mit feuer*

C.   Bellini, *Cavatina*, "Casta Diva" from *Norma*, act 1, scene 4

(continues on next page)

D. Beethoven, Piano Sonata no. 27 in E minor, op. 90, *Mit Lebhaftigkeit und durchaus mit Empfindung und Ausdruck*

Mit Lebhaftigkeit und durchaus mit Empfindung und Ausdruck

E.

F.   Schubert, Ballet music from *Rosamunde*, D. 797

EXERCISE 25.22 Analysis of Modulating Sequences

Bracket and label each of the modulating sequences below. Then, using pivot notation, determine how the last chord of the sequence functions in the new key.

A.   Mozart, Divertimento in B♭ major, K. 254, *Allegro assai*

(continues on next page)

B.　Dvořák, *Cavatina, Romantické kusy (Romantic Pieces)*, op. 75, no. 1, *Allegro moderato*

(continues on next page)

WRITING

EXERCISE 25.23 Figured Bass and Tonicized Areas

Label the harmonies by studying the bass and figures; the appearance of chromaticism in the figures and the bass will help you.

1. Bracket each tonicized area and represent its relation to the main tonic by using a roman numeral.
2. Add upper voices and a first-level roman numeral analysis that relates each of the chords within a tonicization to the expanded harmony.

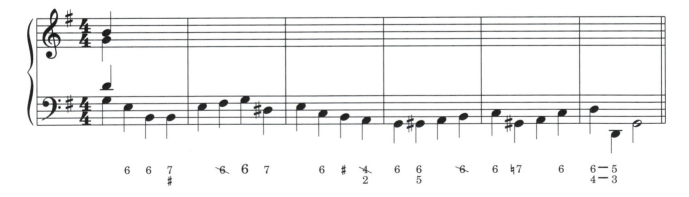

EXERCISE 25.24 Soprano Harmonization

Harmonize each soprano tune below in three different ways. Try to incorporate applied chords, diatonic and applied-chord sequences, and tonicized areas. Begin by breaking up the melodies into harmonic paradigms.

A.

B.

C.

EXERCISE 25.25 Writing Modulating Sequences

Complete the following ordered tasks.

A. Write a progression that
  1. establishes F major
  2. incorporates a diatonic D2 (−5/+4) sequence that breaks off early and becomes a pivot leading to the new key of vi
  3. establishes the key of vi

B. Write a progression in C minor that modulates to III using an A2 (−3/+4) sequence; cadence in the new key.

C. Write a progression in B minor that modulates to iv using a D2 (−5/+4) sequence with applied chords; cadence in the new key.

D. Write a progression that
  1. establishes A major by using a descending bass arpeggiation
  2. modulates to iii by using a sequence of your choice
  3. establishes iii with a step-descent bass
  4. cadences in iii

EXERCISE 25.26 Writing Periods

We are now able to write progressive periods, in keyboard style, in which the closing key is different from the opening key. Further, the use of applied dominant chords will add considerable interest to your compositions. The basic model of the progressive period appears below:

phrase 1: I ⟶ HC (or IAC) in the original key
phrase 2: start in the original key ⟶ PAC in a different, closely related key

A. Write a parallel progressive period that begins in D major and closes in vi.

B. Write a contrasting progressive period that begins in B minor and closes in III.

C. Write a parallel interrupted period in C minor that contains at least four applied chords.

D. Write a parallel sectional period in G minor that contains a tonicization of III within one of the phrases.

E. Write a contrasting progressive period in E♭ that uses a modulating sequence that leads to and closes in V.

F. Write a sentence (phrase or multiphrase type) in A minor that contains a step-descent bass and two tonicized areas of your choice.

EXERCISE 25.27 Figured Bass

Add upper voices to the figured bass below, which modulates by sequence.

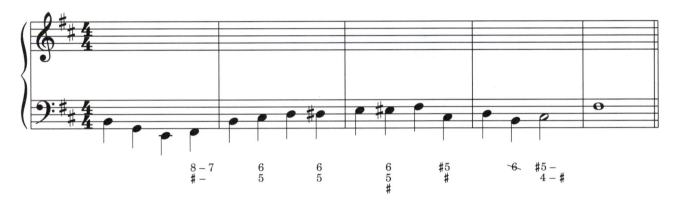

KEYBOARD

EXERCISE 25.28 Modulating Sopranos

Determine the implied initial key and the new key of each soprano fragment. Accidentals will narrow your choices considerably, but since a diatonic melody may modulate without accidentals, there may be more than one harmonic interpretation. Write out the bass line of the cadence and the preceding pre-dominant. Determine a possible bass for the opening of the progression. You will most likely end up in the approximate middle of the fragment, and the one or two unharmonized soprano pitches will be your modulatory pivot. Analyze and add inner voices.

A.   B.

C.

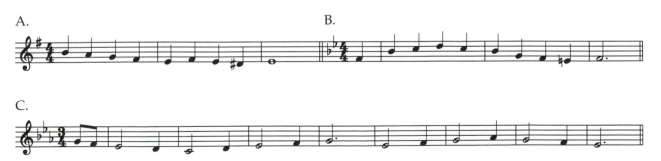

D.   Donizetti, *L'Elisir d'Amore*, act 1, no. 2

LISTENING

EXERCISE 25.29 Dictation: Variations of a Structural Progression

Study each model below. Then listen to and notate the bass and soprano voices and provide roman numerals for the following elaborations of the model. Modulations to closely related keys will occur. Label pivot chords.

Model A

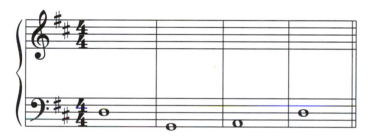

DVD 1
CH 25
TRACK 12

Variation 1   Variation 2

(continues on next page)

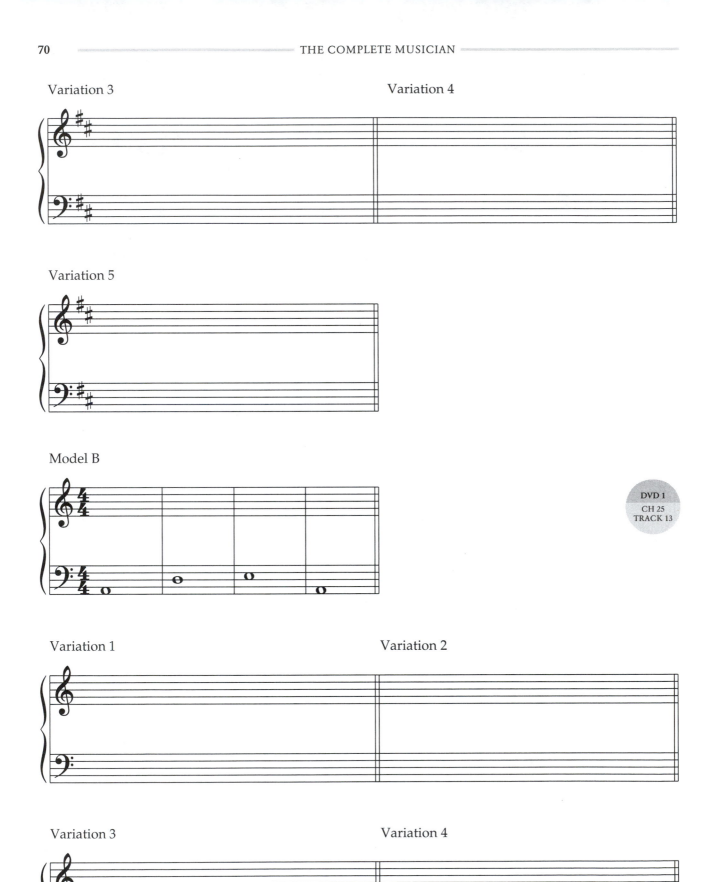

Variation 3

Variation 4

Variation 5

Model B

DVD 1
CH 25
TRACK 13

Variation 1

Variation 2

Variation 3

Variation 4

(continues on next page)

Variation 5

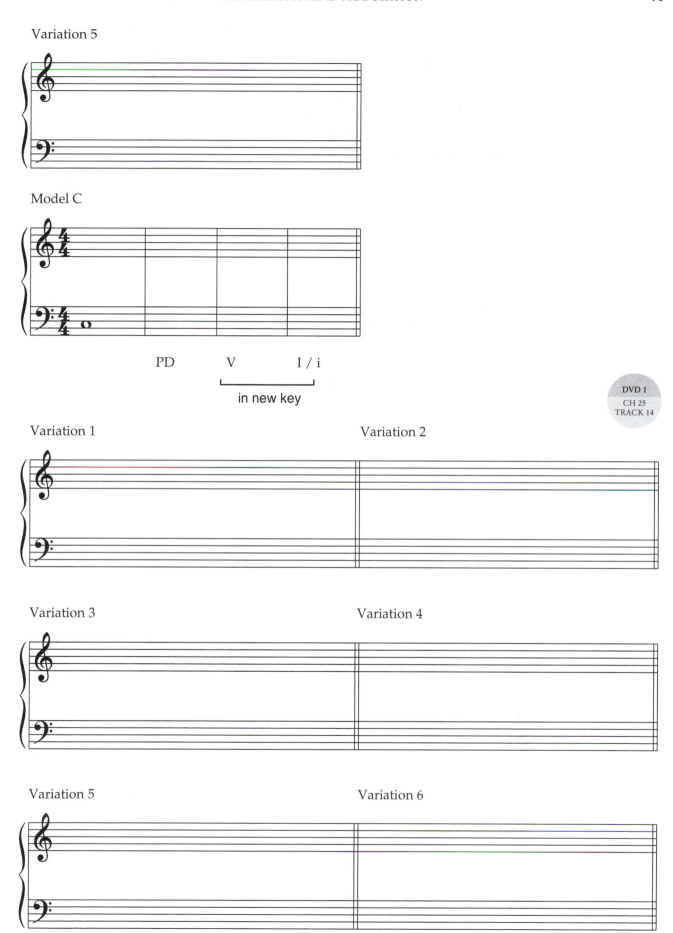

Model C

PD   V   I / i

in new key

DVD 1
CH 25
TRACK 14

Variation 1   Variation 2

Variation 3   Variation 4

Variation 5   Variation 6

Model D

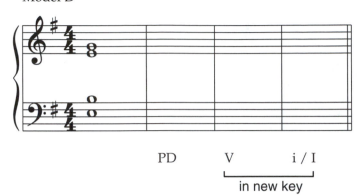

PD   V   i / I

in new key

DVD 1
CH 25
TRACK 15

Variation 1   Variation 2

Variation 3   Variation 4

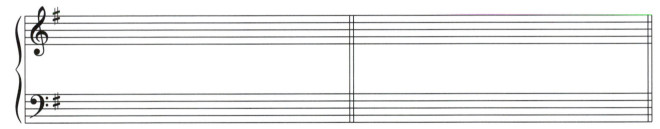

Variation 5

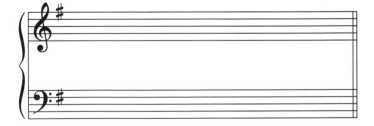

CHAPTER 26

Binary Form and Variation

Assignments for Binary Form

ASSIGNMENT 26.1

ANALYSIS

DVD 1
CH 26
TRACK 1

EXERCISE 26.1

Study each score, provide a formal diagram and label, and answer the accompanying questions.

A. Haydn, String Quartet in B minor, op. 33, no. 1 *Scherzando*
1. Provide a first- and second-level analysis on mm. 1–7.
2. Most of the melodic material in the movement is generated from violin 1's initial tune. Study mm. 1–7, marking motivic patterns between the instruments. Is there a single interval that is particularly important?

(continues on next page)

Fine

B. Türk, "Evening Song"

   1. Provide a diagram for the first period in the piece.

   2. What key is tonicized in mm. 9–10? (Use a roman numeral in relation to the main tonic.) Provide
       roman numerals to represent the work's overall tonal motion.

C. Bach, Sarabande, Lute Suite no. 3 in A minor, BWV 995
    What is the overall tonal structure?

ASSIGNMENT 26.2

ANALYSIS: INSTRUMENTAL DUOS

DVD 1
CH 26
TRACK 2

EXERCISE 26.2

Make a form diagram for each of the following pieces.

A. Mozart, Duet for Two Violins in G major, K. 487

B. Haydn, Trio, Duo in F minor, from Six Duos Concertante for Two Flutes, op. 101, no. 1, Hob. III:25
    Label each suspension in mm. 1–5 and 11–22. Do you find any unprepared dissonance in mm. 1–10?

AURAL ANALYSIS AND NOTATION

DVD 1
CH 26
TRACK 3

EXERCISE 26.3

Beethoven, Trio, Piano Trio no. 8, op. 38 (adapted from his septet, op. 20)

Notate the missing left-hand pitches. Provide a two-level harmonic analysis. Determine the form. What proportional structure does Beethoven employ in mm. 1–8?

(continues on next page)

ASSIGNMENT 26.3

ANALYSIS

DVD 1
CH 26
TRACK 4

EXERCISE 26.4

Make a form diagram for each of the following pieces.

A. Couperin, *Menuet*, Concert Royal no. 1 in G Major for Flute, Oboe, and Basso Continuo

The basso continuo, which is written in the lower two staves, includes two instruments: harpsichord and cello (originally viola da gamba). Thus, even though this is referred to as a trio, there are four players.

1. What is the form?
2. There are many melodic relationships between the instruments.
   a. What is the relationship between the opening winds and the continuo in mm. 1–2? Be specific.
   b. The continuo repeats the winds' material once literally and once in augmentation in the A section. Label these spots.
   c. Starting in m. 9, Couperin develops and intensifies the relationships between the instruments. For example, the descending tune is an inversion of the menuet's opening tune and imitation and pairing of voices occur between all instruments. Find two or three instances of such repetitions.
3. What single key controls mm. 9–16?
4. What is the large-scale tonal progression in mm. 1–20?

A.

(continues on next page)

B.   Kirnberger, Lullaby
There are no repeat signs, but one could say that this piece conforms to the two-reprise, binary-form
idea. Determine a logical place to add the repeat signs. What type of binary form results? Give two or
three reasons why you put the repeats where you did. What harmonic procedure is used in mm. 9–12
(be specific)?

LISTENING

DVD 1
CH 26
TRACK 5

EXERCISE 26.5 Aural Analysis

We now analyze without scores. Begin by studying the questions; then provide a complete formal label.

Beethoven, "Traurig," *Lustig-Traurig,* WoO 54
This short piece is in C minor, in $\frac{3}{8}$ meter. Repeat signs are observed.

1. What type of period occurs in the A section?
2. Notate the bass line of the first four measures on the staff below. You need notate only the "harmonic" (lowest) note of the Alberti figure, which occurs on each measure's downbeat.

ASSIGNMENT 26.4

ANALYSIS

DVD 1
CH 26
TRACK 6

EXERCISE 26.6

Schumann, Romance in B♭ minor, *Three Romances,* op. 28, no. 1

1. Analyze mm. 1–8 and determine the overall tonal progression.
2. Label any sequences you find.
3. The C major is extended from m. 13 to the downbeat of m. 16. What is its harmonic function?

(continues on next page)

DVD 1
CH 26
TRACK 7

LISTENING

EXERCISE 26.7 Aural Analysis

Study the questions that accompany each piece and provide complete formal labels.

A. Purcell, "Ah! How Pleasant 'tis to Love," Z. 353
 1. Notate the opening melody (mm. 1–8) of the piece below with pitch and rhythm (begin by parsing it into phrases).
 2. The upper part of the second section of the piece is given below; notate the bass line and provide a roman numeral analysis.

A.

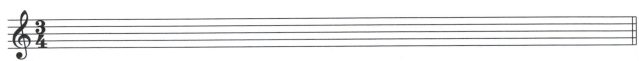

(continues on next page)

B. Haydn, *Menuetto*, Piano Sonata in A major, Hob. XVI:12

This *Menuetto* is in A major, $\frac{3}{4}$ meter.
1. How many phrases are there in the first section (up to the first major cadence)? What are their lengths? Discuss any unusual proportions.
2. Is the melodic material that begins the digression new? If not, from where is it derived?

ASSIGNMENT 26.5

LISTENING

DVD 1
CH 26
TRACK 8

EXERCISE 26.8 Aural Analysis

Study the questions that accompany each piece, and provide complete formal labels.

A. Loeillet, Trio Sonata for Two Violins and Continuo, op. 2, no. 9, *Largo*.
  1. What key is tonicized at the first double bar?
  2. There are two phrases in mm. 1–8. Do they form a period? If so, what type?
  3. Notate the bass line of mm. 1–8 and provide roman numerals. Focus on one phrase at a time, memorizing its entire harmonic progression.
  4. Label the sequences in the second half of the piece in order of appearance.
  5. Are any new keys tonicized in the second half of the piece? If so, what are they?
  6. At what point does the tonic return in the second part of the piece?

A.

B. Mozart, *Menuetto*, String Quartet no. 11 in E♭ major, K. 171
  1. To what key does the first section modulate?
  2. Notate the bass line and provide roman numerals for mm. 1–4 on the staff below.
  3. What contrapuntal technique characterizes the digression?
  4. What harmony is prolonged in the digression?

B.

C. Schubert, *Trio*, Sonatina for Piano and Violin in G minor, op. posth. 127, no. 3, D. 408

  1. Notate the bass line for mm. 1–8 and provide roman numerals.

C.

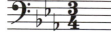

2. Notate the bass line for the digression and provide roman numerals (The starting pitch is G). What harmonic procedure governs the harmony in this section?

3. Finally, notate the rest of the piece (eight measures). You have now notated the harmonic structure for an entire movement; congratulations.

WRITING

EXERCISE 26.9 Composition Projects

A. Warmup. Analyze the antecedent phrase below. Then write a consequent phrase that eventually returns to tonic. Add a melody for any solo instrument or voice.

B. Analyze the antecedent phrase below. Then write a consequent that modulates to III. Include repeat signs at the beginning of the antecedent and the end of the consequent. Write a melody for both phrases that contains a recurring rhythmic or pitch motive. Write another passage of approximately six to eight measures that is sequential and leads to the dominant. Finally, restate the opening eight-measure period, but rewrite the last phrase so that it closes in the tonic. You should end up with a rounded continuous binary form.

Assignments for Variation Form

ASSIGNMENT 26.6

ANALYSIS

DVD 1
CH 26
TRACK 9

EXERCISE 26.10

Below are complete themes and opening passages of two or three of their following variations. For Example A (Handel), only the first section of the theme is given. Study each theme and its variations to determine whether the variation set is continuous or sectional and what musical elements (e.g., harmony, figuration) remain fixed (or only minimally changed) and which are varied. If the theme is sectional, label its overall form (except for Example A, which is incomplete). Begin by providing roman numerals for the theme and studying the melody. Work through each variation, beginning with a harmonic analysis, and then focusing on the varied element. Circle the original components of the melody to see exactly how the composer has altered it in the variations.

A. Handel, *Gavotte*: Keyboard Suite XIV in G major, HWV 222, *Allegro*

Variation 2

B. Mozart, Variations in C major on "Ah, vous dirai-je, Maman," K. 265

THEMA

VAR. I

VAR. II

VAR. III

VAR. VIII

C.   Tommaso Vitali, Variations in G minor

ASSIGNMENT 26.7

ANALYSIS

DVD 1
CH 26
TRACK 11

EXERCISE 26.11

Below are complete themes and opening passages of two or three of their following variations. Study each theme and their variations to determine whether the variation set is continuous or sectional and what musical elements (e.g., harmony, figuration) remain fixed (or only minimally changed) and which are varied. If the theme is sectional, label its overall form. Begin by providing roman numerals for the theme and studying the melody. Work through each variation, focusing on the varied element. Circle the original components of the melody to see exactly how the composer has altered it in the variations.

A. Schubert, Impromptu in B♭ Major, *Four Impromptus for Piano,* op. posth. 142, no. 3, D. 935

B. Mozart, Violin Sonata in G major, K. 379, *Andantino cantabile*

DVD 1
CH 26
TRACK 12

TEMA

Var. III

Var. IV

WRITING

DVD 1
CH 26
TRACK 13

EXERCISE 26.12

Below is the first half of the theme and the incipits of five variations from one of Handel's keyboard works. Analyze the theme and choose three variations whose first half you will complete.

Handel, Air, Keyboard Suite no. III in D minor, HWV 104

Air

(continues on next page)

1. Variation

2. Variation

3. Variation

4. Variation

5. Variation

ASSIGNMENT 26.8

KEYBOARD

EXERCISE 26.13 Aria Pastorella

You will create a small binary piece. Given is the first phrase, which sets the mood and provides you with a model from which the rest of your composition will flow. Think of this binary as a motion to the mediant in m. 8 followed by a drive to the dominant and the subsequent harmonic interruption. The next short section (mm. 13–16) remains entirely in the tonic. Begin by determining the harmonic structure. Measures 1–8 are subdivided into two phrases. You might begin the second phrase in the tonic, but think about moving toward the mediant about halfway through to prepare the cadence in III in m. 8. The material after the double bar might be sequential, leading to the structural dominant. Consider a restatement of the opening material for the final bars, which will create a rounded form and save you time composing new material. Play your solution in four voices, keyboard style. Feel free to include various tones of figuration or simply play broken chord figures throughout. You may even wish to use the figuration as an accompanimental, over which you add a tune.

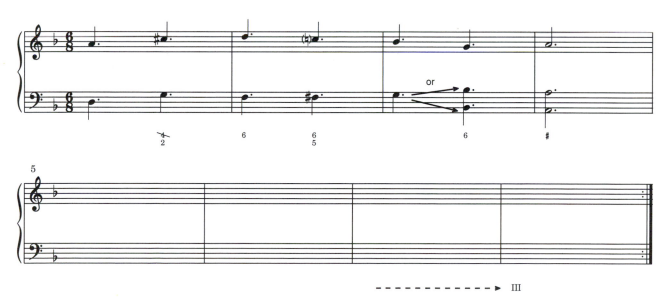

(continues on next page)

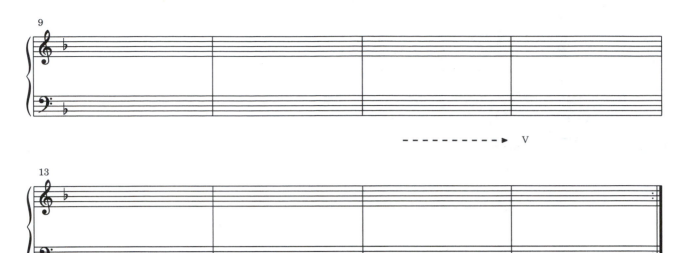

V

i   i

Additional Exercises

WRITING: COMPOSITION

EXERCISE 26.14

Below is the theme from the variation movement of Mozart's G major violin sonata. The opening measures of three variations follow. Analyze the theme and choose two variations to complete, based on their initial texture and accompanimental pattern.

Mozart, *Theme and three variations, on "La bergere Celimène"* for Violin and Piano, K. 359

(continues on next page)

EXERCISE 26.15

Study the themes below, then choose one and write two or three variations on it.

A.   Fischer, "Uranie," *Musikalischer Parnassus*

B.   Haydn, *Tempo di Menuet*, Piano Sonata no. 34 in D major, Hob. XVI:33

EXERCISE 26.16

The theme is given, followed by the first few beats of three variations. Continue the initial texture and accompanimental pattern of each variation. Feel free to write one or more additional variations.

Fischer, "Euterpe," *Musikalischer Parnassus*

THEME

Var. 1

Var. 2

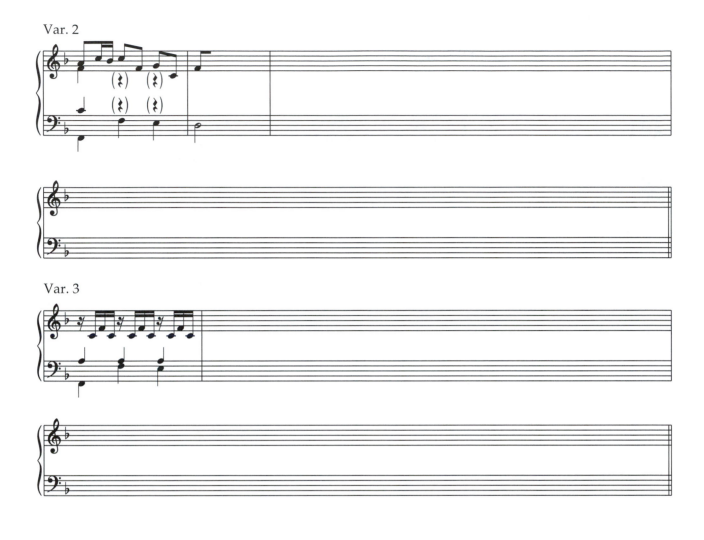

Var. 3

ANALYSIS

DVD 1
CH 26
TRACK 14

EXERCISE 26.17 Binary Form

Analyze the following complete pieces. Answer any accompanying questions.

A.   Galuppi, Sonata in D major, *Adagio*
     To determine the form, consider the unusual proportions in the piece: the material after the first double
     bar occupies fewer measures than the material before the first double bar.

(continues on next page)

B. Fischer, "Uranie: Sarabande," *Musikalischer Parnassus*
    Discuss the overall tonal progression in this piece. Is the D minor harmony that occurs in m. 17 or in m. 22 the true tonal return? What harmonic technique opens the piece? How would you interpret the cadence in m. 8 in terms of the large-scale tonal progression of the piece? Label and discuss any later appearances of this technique.

(continues on next page)

C. Bach, *Menuett* I, Sonata in C major for Flute, BWV 1033

D. Heinichen, Sonata in C minor for Oboe and Bassoon

E. Haydn, Trio, Sonatina in C major, Hob. XVI:7.

Menuet da Capo

CHAPTER 27

Modal Mixture

Exercises for Typical Uses of Melodic and Harmonic Mixture

ASSIGNMENT 27.1

ANALYSIS

EXERCISE 27.1

DVD 1
CH 27
TRACK 1

Analyze the following excerpts from the literature, each of which contains one or more mixture harmonies. Be aware that not all chromatically altered chords indicate mixture; some are applied chords. Recall that mixture harmonies are independent chords that participate in the harmonic progression and usually carry a pre-dominant function. Applied harmonies, on the other hand, function exclusively as dominants, and they lead to their temporary tonics, to which they are subordinate. For mixture harmonies, circle chromatic pitches and label scale degrees.

A. Bach, Chorale, "Vater unser im Himmelreich," BWV 737

B. Mozart, Clarinet Quintet in A major, K. 581, *Allegro*
    What melodic/contrapuntal function does the harmony in m. 4 serve?

E:

C. Mahler, "Die zwei blauen Augen von meinem Schatz" ("The Two Blues Eyes of My Darling"), *Lieder eines fahrenden Gesellen (Songs of a Wayfarer)*, no. 4
    What is the mode of this excerpt? In spite of the pedal that runs through the entire excerpt, one can trace an implied progression of tonic–pre-dominant–dominant–tonic in the excerpt. Mark these functions.

(continues on next page)

stil - ler Nacht wohl __ ü - - ber die dunk - le __ Hal - - de;

D. Beethoven, Violin Sonata no. 9 in A major, "Kreutzer," op. 47, *Adagio sostenuto*
Explore the possibility that Beethoven is introducing modal mixture in stages, first melodically, and then harmonically.

WRITING

EXERCISE 27.2

Complete the varied tasks below.

A. Add upper voices to the bass line; include one example of mixture. Analyze.

B. Complete the progression below in four voices.

C. Realize the figured bass by adding upper voices. Analyze.

A.　　　　　　　　　　　B.　　　　　　　　C.

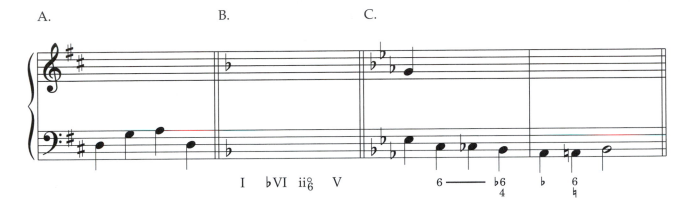

I　♭VI　ii°₆　V

LISTENING

DVD 1
CH 27
TRACK 2

EXERCISE 27.3 Analytical and Aural Identification of Mixture:
                Correction

Listen to the recording, which presents pitch differences from what is notated.
Most of these differences occur on mixture harmonies. Correct the scores to con-
form to what is played. In addition, correct any spelling mistakes (including enharmonic errors). Analyze each progression.

A.

B.

C.

D.

E.

ASSIGNMENT 27.2

LISTENING

EXERCISE 27.4 Differentiation of Diatonic and Mixture Progressions

The major-mode diatonic progressions below are represented by roman numerals. Determine whether the roman numerals correctly represent what you hear, or whether mixture has been invoked. If what is played is what is written, write "OK." If the progressions contain mixture, then amend the roman numerals and figured bass to reflect the chromaticism. For example, given the notated progression I–vi–ii$_6$–V–I, but you hear mixture on both the vi and the ii harmony, you would write "$\flat$VI" and "ii°$_6$."

A. I—ii°$_6$—V$_7$—I _____

B. I—vii°$_6$—I$_6$—IV—V _____

C. I—V—vi—ii$_6$—V—I _____

D. I—vi—IV—V—I _____

E. I—iii—iv—V—vi _____

F. I—V$_6$—IV$_6$—V—vi _____

WRITING

EXERCISE 27.5

Realize the figured bass below in four voices and analyze.

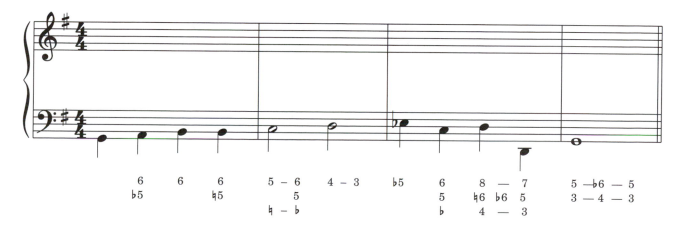

ANALYSIS

DVD 1
CH 27
TRACK 4

EXERCISE 27.6 Analysis

The examples below contain many examples of modal mixture. Analyze each harmony with roman numerals and figured bass. Mixture choices include: minor tonic (i), diminished supertonic (ii°), half diminished supertonic (ii$^{\o6}_5$, ii$^{\o4}_3$), lowered mediant (♭III), minor subdominant (iv$_7$), minor dominant (v), lowered submediant (♭VI).

A.

B.

KEYBOARD

EXERCISE 27.7

Realize the figured bass below by adding inner voices. Analyze.

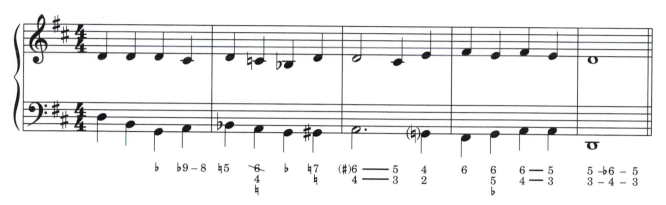

ASSIGNMENT 27.3

WRITING

EXERCISE 27.8 Unfigured Bass

Based on the harmonic implications of the bass, determine a logical chord progression, add inner voices, and analyze. Include as many mixture harmonies as possible.

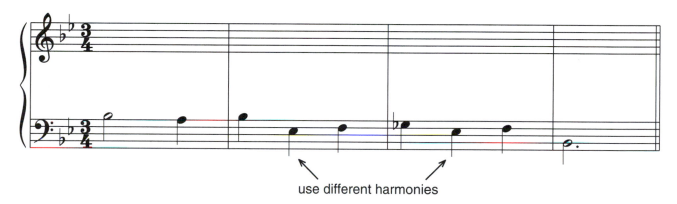

use different harmonies

LISTENING

DVD 1
CH 27
TRACK 5

EXERCISE 27.9

Notate bass and soprano of each progression. Expect one or two examples of modal mixture in each progression. Analyze.

A.   B.

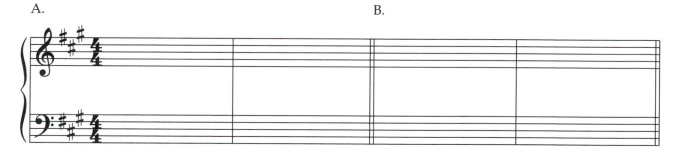

C.

KEYBOARD

EXERCISE 27.10

Complete the tasks below.

A. Play the following progressions in four voices and in two major keys of your choice:

   1. I–ii°$_6$–V$^6_5$ of V—V
   2. I–♭VI–♭iii–ii°$^6_5$–V
   3. I–IV–iv–vii°7 of V–V
   4. I–I6–iv–passing V$^6_4$–iv6–V
   5. I–♭iii–V$^6_5$ of iv–iv–V–I

B. Harmonize the soprano melodies. Include one example of mixture in each.

C. Realize the figured basses by adding upper voices.

D. Harmonize the melody in four voices, adding as many mixture harmonies as possible. Analyze. Asterisks indicate potential mixture harmonies.

Exercises for Chromatic Bass Descents, Plagal Motions, Mixture vs. Applied Chords, and Other Chromatic Chords

ASSIGNMENT 27.4

ANALYSIS

DVD 1
CH 27
TRACK 6

EXERCISE 27.11

Analyze the chromatic bass descents below using roman numerals.

A.

B.   Beethoven, Piano Sonata no. 28 in A major, op. 101, *Lebhaft. Marchmässig*

LISTENING

EXERCISE 27.12

Notate the bass and soprano of each progression. Expect one or two examples of modal mixture in each progression. Analyze.

A.

B.

C.

D.

E.

WRITING

EXERCISE 27.13

Realize the figured bass below.

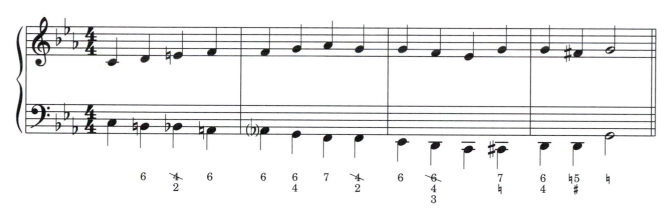

KEYBOARD

EXERCISE 27.14 Plagal Relations and Other Types of Mixture

Play the progressions in major keys up to and including two sharps and flats. Be able to sing the bass while playing the other voices. Optional: in a broken-chord texture improvise on any two examples.

A. I–iv–ii°$^4_3$–I

B. I–iii–IV–iv–I

C. I–vi–IV—iv–cadential six-four–$^\flat$VI

D. I–V$_6$–V$^4_2$ of IV–IV$_6$–iv$_6$–P$^6_4$–ii$^{ø4}_3$–I

ASSIGNMENT 27.5

ANALYSIS

EXERCISE 27.15

Provide roman numerals for the progressions that incorporate III and VI. Be aware that III and VI are often only apparent mixture harmonies (i.e., they may simply be applied chords to vi and ii, respectively).

A.   Beethoven, Piano Trio no. 5 in D major, "Ghost," op. 70, no. 1 *Presto*

B.   Beethoven, Scherzo, Violin Sonata no. 5 in F, major op. 24, "Spring"
What is unusual about the mixture harmony's function in the large-scale tonal framework?

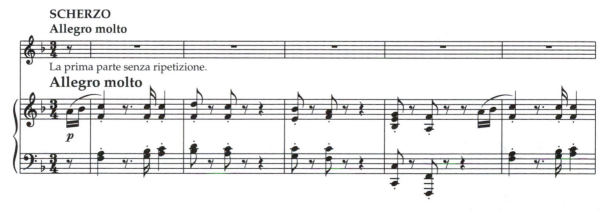

(continues on next page)

C. This example modulates; label the pivot.

WRITING

EXERCISE 27.16

Realize the figured bass below that incorporates plagal relations and III and VI.

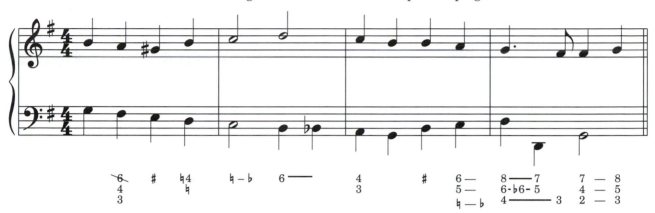

KEYBOARD

EXERCISE 27.17 Potpourri of Mixture Progression

Play the following mixture progressions, which include step-descent bass, plagal relations, and other mixture chords as written, and in major keys up to and including two sharps and flats.

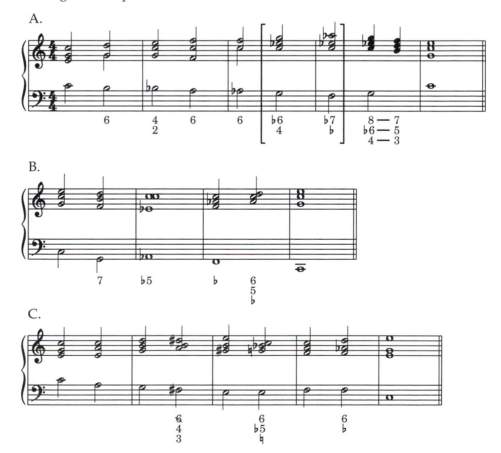

ASSIGNMENT 27.6

LISTENING

EXERCISE 27.18 Analysis and Dictation of Plagal Relations and Other Chords

DVD 1
CH 27
TRACK 8

Notate the bass and provide a roman numeral analysis.

A.

B.

C.

WRITING

EXERCISE 27.19 Plagal Relations, III and VI

Write the following progressions:
A. In E♭ major: I–III–IV–V7–♭VI
B. In B♭ major: I–VI–IV–V–I
C. In F major: I–♭VI–ii°⁶₅–V⁴₂–I6–III–IV–iv♭–I
D. In C major: V–V/♭VI–♭VI–iv♭–V/♭III–♭III–ii°⁶₅–I

EXERCISE 27.20 Composition

Write a 16-measure double period that fleshes out the model below. Choose a meter and melodic structure (parallel or contrasting). Begin in G major and move to its V. Details of each phrase follow.

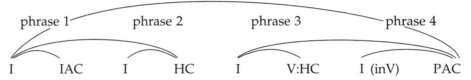

| phrase 1 | phrase 2 | phrase 3 | phrase 4 |

I   IAC   I   HC   I   V:HC   I (inV)   PAC

Phrase 1: Include a sequence of your choice that uses suspensions.
Phrase 2: Include one applied chord and one example of mixture.
Phrase 3: Use a mixture harmony to lead to the HC in V.
Phrase 4: Include a step-descent bass.

Additional Exercises

WRITING

EXERCISE 27.21 Melody Harmonization

Harmonize the following melody in G major; add as many mixture harmonies as possible. Your choices are ii°$^6_5$, ♭III, III, iv, ♭VI, and VI. Try playing your solution. Then add the bass and, finally, the inner voices. Analyze.

EXERCISE 27.22 Illustrations

Complete the following tasks in four voices.
A. Modulate from D major to its dominant. Cast the progression in two phrases to create a period—the type is left up to you. Include a suspension and an example of mixture in both the original key and the dominant key.
B. Modulate from F major to its diatonic submediant. Include a proper use of ♭III in the original key and a lament bass in the new key.
C. Modulate from C minor to its VI. Include at least two applied chords in the original key and two suspensions and an example of mixture in the new key.

KEYBOARD

EXERCISE 27.23 Review

The following exercises review sequences, harmonization, tonicization, and modulation.
A. Harmonize each bass and soprano scale degree pattern in three different ways. Use a mix of major and minor keys. Be able to sing the given patterns while playing the other three voices.

Bass scale degree patterns:
1̂–2̂–3̂–7̂–1̂   1̂–2̂–3̂–4̂–5̂   1̂–6̂–4̂–5̂–1̂   1̂–♯1̂–2̂–3̂–4̂–♯4̂–5̂

Soprano scale degree patterns:
1̂–7̂–1̂–2̂–3̂–4̂–5̂   5̂–6̂–5̂–4̂–3̂–2̂–1̂   1̂–♭7̂–6̂–5̂–4̂–♯4̂–5̂

B. Determine the type of sequence implied from the given soprano scale degrees. Play it in four voices in any two major and minor keys. Be able to sing the given patterns while playing the other three voices.
1. $\hat{3}$–$\hat{4}$–$\hat{2}$–$\hat{3}$–$\hat{1}$–$\hat{2}$–$\hat{7}$–$\hat{1}$
2. $\hat{3}$–$\hat{2}$–$\hat{1}$–$\hat{7}$–$\hat{6}$–$\hat{5}$–$\hat{4}$
3. $\hat{5}$–$\hat{6}$–$\hat{4}$–$\hat{5}$–$\hat{3}$–$\hat{4}$–$\hat{2}$–$\hat{3}$
4. ($\hat{5}$)–$\hat{5}$–$\hat{4}$–$\hat{6}$–$\hat{5}$–b$\hat{7}$–$\hat{6}$
5. $\hat{1}$–#$\hat{1}$–$\hat{2}$–#$\hat{2}$–$\hat{3}$–$\hat{3}$–$\hat{4}$

C. Determine the type of sequence implied from the given bass scale degrees. Play it in four voices in any two major and minor keys:
1. $\hat{1}$–$\hat{6}$–$\hat{7}$–$\hat{5}$–$\hat{6}$–$\hat{4}$–$\hat{5}$–$\hat{3}$
2. $\hat{1}$–#$\hat{1}$–$\hat{2}$–#$\hat{2}$–$\hat{3}$–$\hat{3}$–$\hat{4}$
3. $\hat{1}$–$\hat{5}$–$\hat{6}$–$\hat{3}$–$\hat{4}$–$\hat{1}$
4. $\hat{1}$–$\hat{7}$–$\hat{6}$–$\hat{5}$–$\hat{4}$

EXERCISE 27.24 Review: Modulation

Complete the following tasks.
A. Using 8 to 10 chords, modulate from I to iii in D major, from I to V in A major, and from i to III in G minor.
B. You are given the following series of harmonies in the key of F major: F major, G minor, A minor, and B♭ major. Using each as a pivot, modulate to as many different diatonic keys as possible. For example, a C major triad in F major (V) can become a pivot chord that leads to the keys of C major, D minor, E minor, G major, and A minor.

EXERCISE 27.25 Review: Applied Chords

Complete the following tasks on a keyboard.
A. Incorporate the progression V7/vi to vi in the keys of D major and G minor.
B. Incorporate the progression vii°7/V to V in the keys of E♭ major and A major.
C. Play a D3 sequence incorporating applied chords in the keys of B♭ major and C minor.
D. Play an A2 sequence incorporating applied chords in the key of E major.

EXERCISE 27.26 Review: Illustrations

Complete the following tasks on a separate sheet of manuscript paper.
A. Modulate from I to V in C major; include
1. two suspensions
2. any sequence
B. Modulate from i to III in E minor; include
1. a D2 sequence
2. a passing six-four and cadential six-four
3. a 9–8 suspension
C. Modulate from i to v in A minor; include
1. a lament bass
2. two applied chords
3. a bass suspension

EXERCISE 27.27 Review: Figured Bass: Mixture and Applied Chords

Realize the figured bass in four voices. Analyze.

EXERCISE 27.28 Review: Unfigured Bass, Tonicization, and Modulation

Realize the unfigured bass (with given soprano) in four voices. Be able to sing either given voice while playing the other three voices. Analyze.

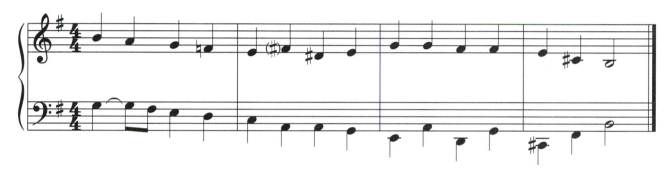

EXERCISE 27.29 Recipes

Below are two sets of ingredients for making two satisfying main-course progressions that incorporate mixture. However, they appear in a jumbled order; you will need to place them in a logical order before combining them into a finished product.

Recipe 1	Recipe 2
Take one PAC with suspension	One teaspoon of ♭VI
Slowly spread one step-descent bass	Prolong tonic with bass arpeggiation
Place in the key of D major	Sprinkle in two suspensions
Add a dash of ♭III	Close with tonicization of III
Tonicize any closely related key	Begin in C minor
Add a measure or two of A2 (−3/+4) sequence	Knead in one passing six-four chord
Mix the ingredients in $\frac{4}{4}$ meter	Gently add one D2 (−5/+4) sequence
This batch will fit in a 6 to 10-measure baking pan	Place in an 8-measure triple meter oven-proof container

Expansion of Modal Mixture Harmonies: Chromatic Modulation and the German *Lied*

ASSIGNMENT 28.1

ANALYSIS

DVD 1
CH 28
TRACK 1

EXERCISE 28.1

Listen to the following examples of prepared (i.e., pivot chord) chromatic tonicizations. Then do the following.

1. Locate and label the chromatic tonicization.
2. Locate and interpret the pivot chord or pivot area.
3. Use roman numerals to write out the overall harmonic progression.

Note: You do *not* need to analyze every harmony.
Two sample solutions are provided.

Sample solution 1

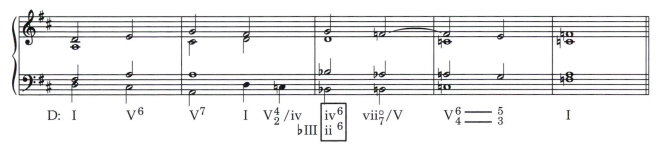

Sample solution 2: Beethoven, Violin Sonata, op. 24, "Spring," *Adagio molto espressivo*

A.

B.

C.   Beethoven, Piano Sonata no. 2 in A major, op. 2, no. 2, *Largo appassionato*

WRITING

EXERCISE 28.2 Figured Bass

Realize the figured bass below in four voices and analyze.

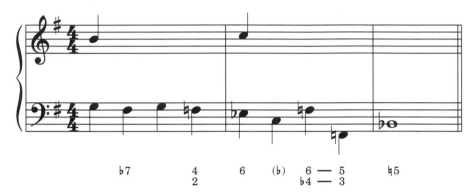

b7   4   6   (b) 6 — 5   ♮5
          2   b4 — 3

LISTENING

DVD 1
CH 28
TRACK 2

EXERCISE 28.3 Analysis/Dictation

Below are two score examples, each of which modulates. The bass lines, however, are mostly missing.

1. Listen to each example, then notate the bass.
2. Provide roman numerals, circling any pivots. Watch carefully for motions to the following keys:

   in major keys: ♭III, iii, V, ♭VI, vi
   in minor keys: III, v, VI

A.

B.

ASSIGNMENT 28.2

ANALYSIS

DVD 1
CH 28
TRACK 3

EXERCISE 28.4

Listen to the following examples of prepared (i.e., pivot chord) chromatic tonicizations. Then do the following.

1. Locate and label the chromatic tonicization.
2. Locate and interpret the pivot chord or pivot area.
3. Use roman numerals to write out the overall harmonic progression.

Note: You do *not* need to analyze every harmony.

A.

B. Mozart, String Quartet in A major, K. 464, *Allegro*
    What type of formal construction occurs in mm. 1–16?

(continues on next page)

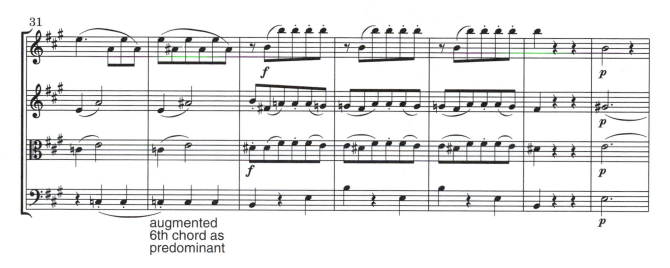

augmented
6th chord as
predominant

WRITING

EXERCISE 28.5

Realize the figured bass below in four voices and analyze.

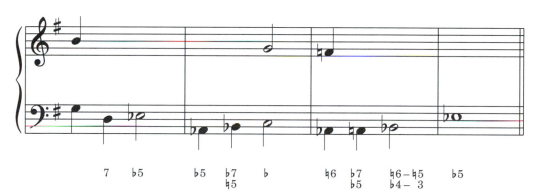

KEYBOARD

EXERCISE 28.6 Soprano Harmonization

Harmonize the soprano fragments below, each of which implies a chromatic modulation. The destinations include ♭VI, bIII, VI, and III.

A.

B.

C.

ASSIGNMENT 28.3

LISTENING

DVD 1
CH 28
TRACK 4

EXERCISE 28.7 Analysis/Dictation

Below are two score examples, each of which modulates. The bass lines, however, are partially or completely missing.

1. Listen to each example, then notate the bass.
2. Provide roman numerals, circling any pivots. Watch carefully for motions to the following keys:

in major keys: ♭III, iii, III, V, ♭VI, vi, VI
in minor keys: III, v, VI

A.

B.

WRITING

EXERCISE 28.8 Melody Harmonization

Harmonize the soprano melodic fragments below in four voices, each of which implies a chromatic tonicization. Analyze with roman numerals and mark the pivot carefully.

A.

B.

C.

D.

KEYBOARD

EXERCISE 28.9

Realize in four voices the following figured bass. Analyze. Be able to sing either outer voice while playing the remaining voices.

Exercises for Unprepared and Common-Tone Modulations, and the German Lied

ASSIGNMENT 28.4

WRITING

EXERCISE 28.10 Multiple Harmonizations of a Soprano Melody

Below are two modulating soprano melodies that may be harmonized in a variety of ways. Analyze and add a bass line. *You need not add inner voices.*

A.

B.

ANALYSIS

EXERCISE 28.11 Prepared and Common-Tone Chromatic Modulations

Below are two types of chromatic third modulations: pivot chord and common tone.

1. Use roman numerals to label the chromatic destination.
2. Determine whether Chopin has used a pivot chord modulation (in which a mixture chord in the first key becomes a diatonic chord in the new key) or a common-tone modulation (a single pitch is reinterpreted in the new key). If you encounter a pivot chord modulation, mark the pivot. If you encounter a common-tone modulation, circle and beam the common pitch class(es).

A. Chopin, Etude in Ab major, op. 10, no. 10

B. Brahms, "Die Mainacht" ("The May Night"), *Viér ernste Gesänge (Four Serious Songs)*, op. 43, no. 2
Consider B major to be an enharmonic respelling of C♭ major.

(continues on next page)

Ü - ber - hül - let von Laub

p

LISTENING

DVD 1
CH 28
TRACK 6

EXERCISE 28.12 Notation of Chromatic Modulations

The following examples modulate either to ♭III or ♭VI. On a separate sheet of manuscript paper, notate the bass and soprano; provide roman numerals. Remember, the standard modulatory technique establishes the initial key, employs a pivot (using a mixture chord as a pre-dominant), establishes the new key, and closes with a PAC. Exercises A and B have two sharps and are in $\frac{4}{4}$. Exercise C has one sharp and is in $\frac{4}{4}$. Exercise D has one sharp and is in $\frac{3}{4}$. Exercise E has two sharps and is in $\frac{6}{8}$.

WRITING

EXERCISE 28.13 Common-Tone and Other Types of Modulation

Complete the following tasks using five to seven chords and in four voices; analyze.

A. Modulate from C major to A♭ major by means of a common-tone modulation.

B. Modulate from E major to ♭III by means of a common-tone modulation.

C. Modulate from B♭ major to D major by means of a mixture chord pivot.

D. Modulate from A major to F major, using any sequence as a pivot.

E. Given an F minor triad as a pivot, modulate from:

1. C major to A♭ major
2. E♭ major to C minor
3. A♭ major to F minor

ASSIGNMENT 28.5

LISTENING

DVD 1
CH 28
TRACK 7

EXERCISE 28.14 Analysis/Dictation

The examples below from the literature include chromatic modulations. Identify pivots when appropriate. Only a few bass notes are included; notate the remaining bass notes and provide roman numerals.

A. Beethoven, "Dimmi, ben mio" ("Hoffnung"), *Vier Arietten*, op. 82, no. 1

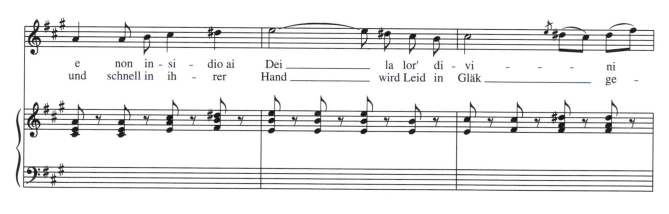

(continues on next page)

B.   Wagner, *Das Rheingold*, scene 2

WRITING

EXERCISE 28.15

Realize the unfigured bass and soprano melody in four voices. Analyze. Sing either outer voice while playing the other voices.

ASSIGNMENT 28.6

INTERACTIVE ANALYSIS

DVD 1
CH 28
TRACK 8

EXERCISE 28.16

Schubert, "An Emma" ("To Emma"), D. 311c

This song presents chromatic third relations prepared by modal mixture. Study the text and listen to the song. Then, analyze to the best of your ability, using roman numerals. Star any passages whose resolutions or progressions you find puzzling or interesting. Then, attempt a second analysis with the following leading discussion guiding you.

(continues on next page)

Flam - me   Him - mels-gluth,   stirbt sie   wie ein ir - disch Gut?

Weit in nebelgrauer Ferne	Far in the great misty distance
Liegt mir das vergangne Glück,	lies my past happiness.
Nur an einem schönen Sterne	My gaze still lingers fondly
Weilt mit Liebe noch der Blick.	on one lovely star alone;
Aber, wie des Sternes Pracht,	but the splendor of the star,
Ist es nur ein Schein der Nacht.	it is only an illusion of the night.
Deckte dir der lange Schlummer,	If the long sleep of night
Dir der Tod die Augen zu,	had closed your eyes
Dich besässe doch mein Kummer,	my grief might still possess you;
Meinem Herzen lebtest du.	you would live on in my heart.
Aber ach! du lebst im Licht,	But oh, you live in the light,
Meiner Liebe lebst du nicht.	but you do not live for my love.
Kann der Liebe süss Verlangen,	Emma, can love's sweetness
Emma, kann's vergänglich sein?	fade and die?
Was dahin ist und vergangen,	That which is past and gone,
Emma, kann's die Liebe sein?	Emma—can that be love?
Ihrer Flamme Himmelsgluth,	Can the heavenly glow of its ardor die,
Stirbt sie wie ein irdisch Gut?	like some earthly possession?

(trans. John Reed, *The Schubert Song Companion*)

The goal of *Lied* analysis is to figure out how the musical relations you find may be aligned with the underlying poetic drama. The subject of this poem is timeless. A jilted lover reflecting on happier times is jarred back repeatedly to the reality of his loss. The rhyme scheme of the text is ababcc. The last two lines of each strophe are segregated both by rhyme scheme and meaning, acting as a refrain. In the first two strophes, this refrain and the preceding verse are set in opposition to each other. The verse expresses the protagonist's longing for love, while the refrain redirects this thought toward the painful truth. The first verse emphasizes past happiness, and the distance between the speaker and the object of his gaze, the star, is symbolic of the time that separates him from the object of his affection, Emma.

1. Are particular words highlighted in the musical setting? By what means? Consider the use of accidentals, chromatic harmony, and dramatic pause.
2. Locate all the A major triads. Are certain words associated with this chord and with D minor (its resolution chord)?
3. Are there harmonic progressions left incomplete? How might these interact with the text?
4. In the second verse (mm. 20ff), consider the analogy of death with night and slumber. Is the beloved dead, or only dead to the love of the speaker?
5. Is there a change in the speaker's perspective? Where is the climax in this section? In the closing verse, the speaker poses a question to his beloved: If true love can never die, and that which we shared has, then how could it have been love? Why is there the curious sojourn into A♭ major?

ASSIGNMENT 28.7

COMPARATIVE ANALYSIS

DVD 1
CH 28
TRACK 9

EXERCISE 28.17

Analyze the excerpts below from Beethoven's and Schubert's settings of Goethe's poem "Kennst du das Land?" Focus on chromaticism that results from tonicization and modal mixture. Then, study the two text settings, and compare and contrast the way Beethoven and Schubert have merged text and music.

A. Beethoven, "Mignon," Op. 75, no. 1

(continues on next page)

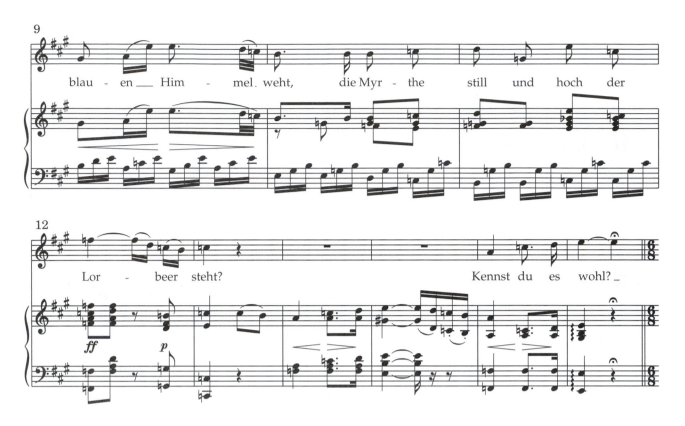

blau - en __ Him - mel. weht, die Myr - the still und hoch der Lor - beer steht? Kennst du es wohl? _

B.　Schubert, "Kennst du das Land?" ("Mignons Gesang") ("Do you know the Land?"), D.321

Mässig

Kennst du das Land, _ wo die Ci - tro - nen blühn, im dunk - len Laub die
Kennst du das Haus? _ Auf Säu - len ruht sein Dach, es glänzt der Saal, es

Gold - O - ran - gen glühn, ein sanf - ter _ Wind vom
schim - mert das __ Ge - mach, und Mar - mor - bil - der

(continues on next page)

Kennst du das Land, wo die Zitronen blühn,
Im dunkeln Laub die Gold-Orangen glüh'n,
Ein sanfter Wind vom blauen Himmel weht,
Die Myrthe still und hoch der Lorbeer steht?
Kennst du es wohl? . . .
Kennst du das Haus? Auf Säulen ruht sein Dach,
Es glänzt der Saal, es schimmert das Gemach,
Und Marmorbilder stehn und sehn mich an:
Was hat man dir, du armes Kind, getan?
Kennst du es wohl?. . .

Do you know where the lemon grows,
In dark foliage the golden-orange glows,
A gentle breeze blows from the blue sky,
Do the myrtle and the laurel, stand high?
Do you know it well? . . .
Do you know the the house, its roof on columns fine?
Its hall glows brightly and its chambers shine,
And marble figures stand and gaze at me;
What have they done, oh poor child, to you?
Do you know it well? . . .

Additional Exercises

WRITING

EXERCISE 28.18 Melody Harmonization

Complete the following tasks.

1. Add a bass line to the melody below.
2. Include a first- and second-level analysis
3. Mark any modulations and pivot chords.
4. In addition:

    A. m. 1–beat 1 of m. 2: expand the tonic
    B. m. 2: use mixture
    C. m 3: use mixture
    D. m. 4: use an applied chord
    E. m. 7: use a deceptive motion in the new key
    F. m. 8: close in the new key with a PAC

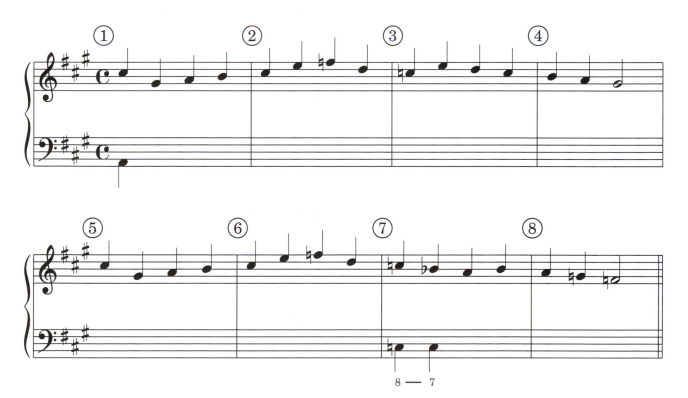

WRITING

EXERCISE 28.19 Harmonizing Soprano Fragments: Review

Harmonize the following soprano fragments and complete any required tasks. Then, provide roman numerals, work out a good bass line, and add inner voices.

A.

B.

C.

A. Include
1) tonicization
2) diminished seventh chord

B. Include
1) at least one example of tonicization
2) one example of mixture

C. Include
1) a sequence
2) an applied °7 chord
3) a modulation (close in new tonal area)

KEYBOARD

EXERCISE 28.20 Illustrations

Complete the following tasks in four voices.

A. Given the key of D major, use iv as a pivot to tonicize ♭III.

B. Given the key of D major, use iv as a pivot to tonicize ♭VI.

C. Given the key of C major, use ♭VI as a pivot to tonicize ♭III.

D. Modulate from G major to ♭III. Include two suspensions and a sequence.

EXERCISE 28.21 Pitch Reinterpretation

Follow the instructions below to construct chromatic tonicizations. Each progression should contain approximately 12 chords.

A. Modulate from D major to B♭ major; use $\hat{1}$ in the original key as the common-note pivot. Include one applied chord and two six-four chords.

B. Modulate from F major to A♭; use $\hat{5}$ in the original key as the common-note pivot. Include one voice exchange and one nondominant seventh chord.

C. Modulate from G major to E♭ major; use a common-chord pivot (it must be a mixture chord in the first key). Begin with an EPM (embedded phrase model) and include two suspensions within the progression.

D. Modulate from C major to E major; use a common-chord pivot (it must be a mixture chord in the first key). Include a step-descent bass.

E. Modulate from F major to A major; use $\hat{3}$ in the original key as the common-note pivot. Include an example of modal mixture in each key.

ANALYSIS

DVD 1
CH 28
TRACK 10

EXERCISE 28.22

The examples below from the literature include chromatic modulations. Identify pivots when appropriate and provide roman numerals.

A. Chopin, Mazurka in A♭ major, op. 17, no. 3

B. Brahms, "Wenn ich mit Menschen" *Vier ernste Gesänge* (*Four Serious Songs*), op. 121, no. 4

CHAPTER 29

The Neapolitan Sixth Chord (♭II6)

Exercises for Identification, Writing, and Hearing

ASSIGNMENT 29.1

ANALYSIS

DVD 1
CH 29
TRACK 1

EXERCISE 29.1

Analyze the following short examples, each of which contains the Neapolitan chord.

A. Meyerbeer, "Scirocco"

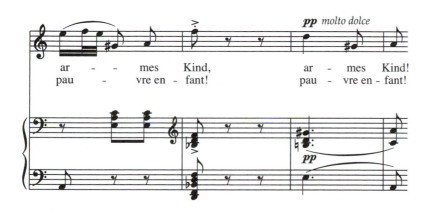

B.　Beethoven, "Sehnsucht," WoO 134

Nur　　wer die Sehn - sucht kennt　weiss, was　ich lei　-　de!
Ach!　　der mich liebt　und kennt　ist in　der Wei　-　te.

C.

D.　Brahms, Clarinet Sonata in F minor, op 120

E.　Wagner, "Leb Wohl," *Die Walküre*, Act 3, Scene 3

leb'　　wohl!

(continues on next page)

leb'   wohl!

LISTENING

DVD 1
CH 29
TRACK 2

EXERCISE 29.2

Notate the bass voice in the following six short progressions (*c.* six chords per progression). Include roman numerals. Note: Pre-dominants include ii°, ♭II6, iv, and iv6; progressions may open with an EPM.

A.

B.

C.

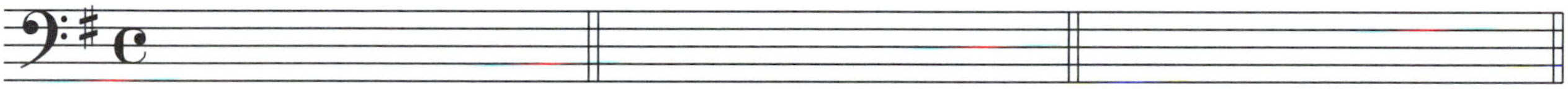

D.

E.

F.

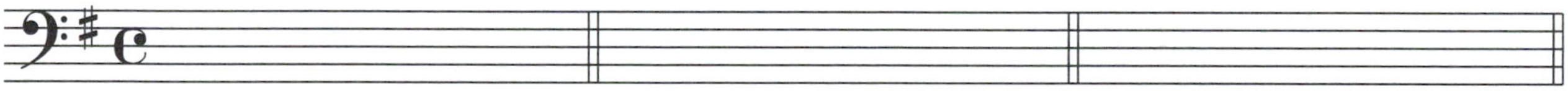

WRITING

EXERCISE 29.3 Spelling, Identifying, and Writing ♭II6

Given the following triads, determine the minor key in which each triad functions as ♭II6 and provide a key signature. Then, resolve each as required. You will need to correct the two misspelled Neapolitan harmonies (only one of the members of the chord is misspelled).

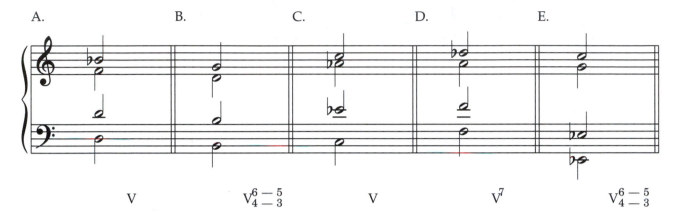

EXERCISE 29.4

Realize in four voices the following figured basses. Analyze.

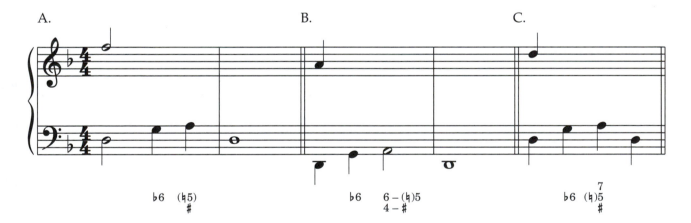

ASSIGNMENT 29.2

WRITING

EXERCISE 29.5 More Spelling, Identifying, and Writing ♭II6

Given is the bass of ♭II6 chords in various keys. Determine the key for each example, and provide a key signature. Then, complete the ♭II6 chord in four voices (double the bass in each case) and precede and follow it as required.

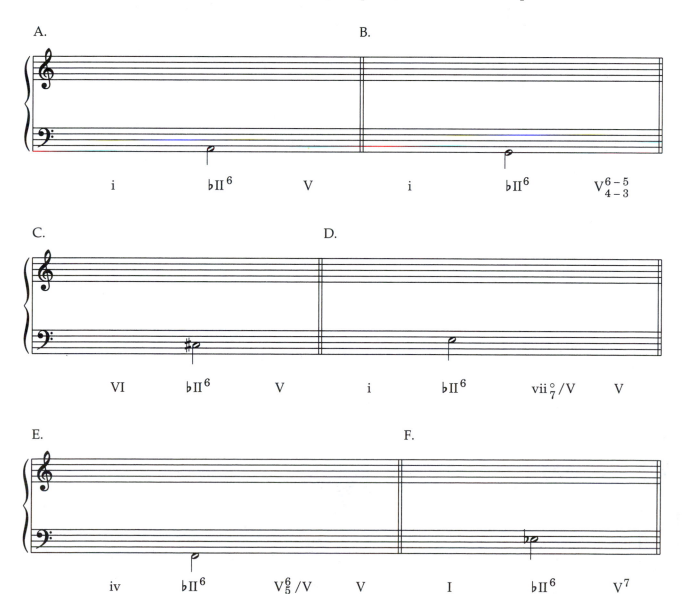

A.

i   ♭II^6 V

B.

i   ♭II^6 V$^{6-5}_{4-3}$

C.

VI   ♭II^6 V

D.

i   ♭II^6 vii°^{7}/V   V

E.

iv   ♭II^6 V$^6_5$/V   V

F.

I   ♭II^6 V^7

EXERCISE 29.6

Realize the figured bass below; analyze.

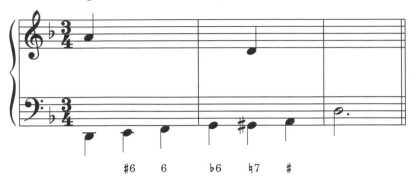

LISTENING

DVD 1
CH 29
TRACK 3

EXERCISE 29.7 Bass Notation

Listen to and study each example, the upper voices for which are given. Notate the bass line and provide roman numerals for each. Arrows indicate where to notate bass notes.

A. Schubert, "Am See" ("By the Lake"), D.124

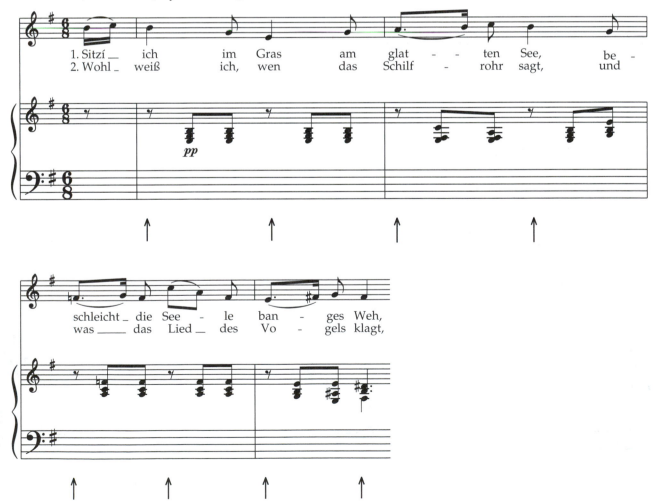

B. Chopin, Waltz in A minor, Op. 34, no. 2, BI 64

ASSIGNMENT 29.3

WRITING

EXERCISE 29.8 Harmonic Progressions

Choose a suitable meter and rhythmic setting and write the following progressions in four voices. Analyze. Optional: Play your progressions on the piano in keyboard style. Be able to sing either upper voice while playing the remaining three voices.

A. D minor: i–VI–♭II6–V–i

B. B minor: i–vii°6–i6–♭II6–vii°7/V–V–I

C. C minor: i–V6/III–III–♭II6–cad. 6/4–5/3–i

EXERCISE 29.9 Melodic Fragments

Write a logical bass line, analyze, add inner voices. The Neapolitan must appear at least once in each exercise.

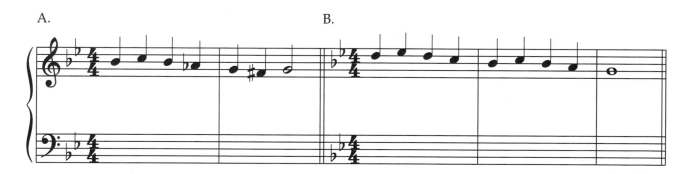

LISTENING

DVD 1
CH 29
TRACK 4

EXERCISE 29.10 Bass Notation

Listen to and study each example, the upper voices for which are given. Notate the bass line and provide roman numerals for each. Arrows indicate where to notate bass pitches.

A. Schumann, "Hör' ich das Liedchen klingen" ("I Hear the Dear Song Sounding"), *Dichterliebe*, op. 48, no. 10
   This example contains a tonicization of iv.

B.   Dvorak, *Dumka*, from Piano Quintet in A major, op. 81, ii

C.   Schumann, String Quartet no. 3 in A major, *Assai agitato*

ASSIGNMENT 29.4

WRITING

EXERCISE 29.11

Realize the figured bass and given melody below by adding inner voices. Analyze.
What type of progression opens the exercise?

KEYBOARD

EXERCISE 29.12

Harmonize the short soprano melodies in two different ways, one of which must
include an example of ♭II6. Hint: Both settings may not need to be in minor. Feel
free to include applied harmonies and mixture. Analyze.

LISTENING

DVD 1
CH 29
TRACK 5

EXERCISE 29.13

Determine whether the progression you hear contains a single harmonic motion or is divided into two or more subphrases. If it is divided, determine each subphrase's function (e.g., to prolong the tonic). Analyze with roman numerals; bracket and label sequences. Then, listen again and sing the bass and notate it. You may encounter a modulation to a closely related key.

A.

B.

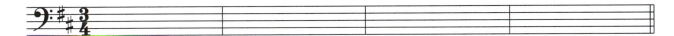

C.

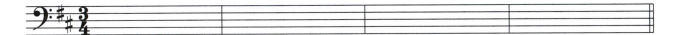

ASSIGNMENT 29.5

WRITING:

EXERCISE 29.14 Unfigured Bass and Melody

Based on the harmonic implications of the bass and soprano, add inner voices and analyze.

EXERCISE 29.15 Illustration

Determine a logical ordering of the musical elements below, then incorporate them into a progression in four voices. Analyze your work. Note: You may be able to combine two or more steps.

In the key of E minor, write a progression in 6/8 that

1. tonicizes III
2. includes a neighbor motive; it should occur in various contexts, either harmonized or unharmonized as a nonharmonic tone
3. includes an example of mixture in the new key
4. includes a sequence of your choice in either key
5. an example of ♭II6 in the first key

KEYBOARD

EXERCISE 29.16

Realize in four voices and analyze the figured bass below using two levels. Be able to sing the bass while playing the upper voices.

ANALYSIS

EXERCISE 29.17

LONGER ANALYTIC PROJECT

Locatelli, Sonata no. 3 in G minor, *Twelve Sonatas for Flute and Continuo,*
Largo

1. What is the form of this piece?
2. The interval of the third, especially encompassing $\hat{1}$–$\hat{3}$, is very important throughout the piece. Mark various statements of the third. Explore how thirds in multiple voices may occur simultaneously, creating voice exchanges and other interesting contrapuntal motions.
3. A progressive period occurs in the A section. Analyze the pivot area. Compare this pivot with that which leads back to the tonic at the end of the digression.
4. Label all sequences.
5. Perform a roman numeral analysis of mm. 1–4.

LISTENING

EXERCISE 29.18 Notation of Progressions Incorporating
the Neapolitan

Provide roman numerals and notate both bass and soprano.

A.

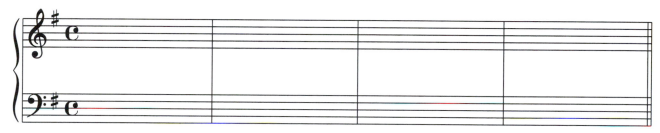

B.

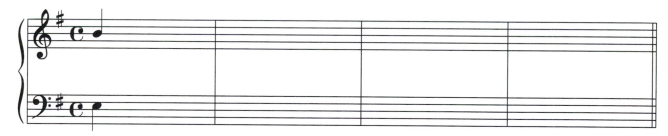

C.

ASSIGNMENT 29.6

DVD 1
CH 29
TRACK 8

LISTENING

EXERCISE 29.19 The Expanded Neapolitan in Homophonic Settings

Provide roman numerals and a bass line for the following examples.

A.

B.

C.

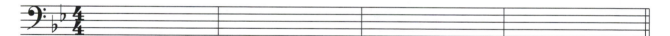

D.

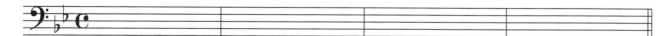

WRITING

EXERCISE 29.20 Soprano Harmonization

Harmonize in four voices the following soprano melodies. Look for opportunities to incorporate the Neapolitan, mixture harmonies, and sequences. Analyze. Optional: Be able to play your progressions on the piano.

A.

B.

KEYBOARD

EXERCISE 29.21

Complete the unfigured bass with soprano in four voices. Be aware of expansions of ♭II. Analyze.

Additional Exercise

LISTENING

EXERCISE 29.22   Notation of Phrases Incorporating the Neapolitan

Determine whether the progression you hear contains a single harmonic motion or is divided into two or more subphrases. If it is divided, determine each subphrase's function (e.g., to prolong the tonic). Analyze with roman numerals; bracket and label sequences. Then, listen again and sing the bass and notate it. You may encounter a modulation to a closely related key.

A.

B.

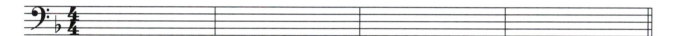

C.

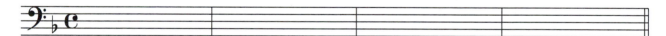

D.

EXERCISE 29.23   Notation of Progressions Incorporating the Neapolitan

Provide roman numerals and notate both bass and soprano for Exercises A–E, each of which is four measures. Exercise F, from the literature, occupies eight measures; notate only the bass and analyze.

A.

B.

C.

D.

E.

F.   Vivaldi, Concerto in C major for Two Violins, F.XI/44, Ry 114, P27, Ri 493.

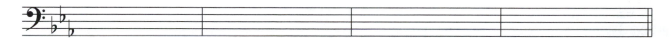

EXERCISE 29.24 The Expanded Neapolitan in Figuration

DVD 1
CH 29
TRACK 11

Notate the bass voice and provide roman numerals for the following figurated examples of expanded Neapolitans; the last one is taken from the literature.

A.

B.

C.

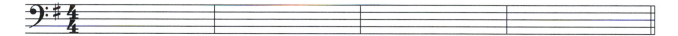

D.

E.   Schubert, *Trio*, Violin Sonata in A minor, Op. posth. 137, no. 2, D. 385

EXERCISE 29.25 Phrase Model Expansions

Study the given tonal model, which is followed by a series of variations and expansions that flesh out the model's harmonic progression. Each variation occupies two to four measures. Notate the outer voices and analyze each of the expansions.

Phrase model 1

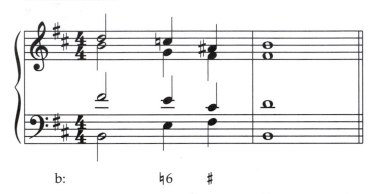

b: ♮6   ♯

Expansion 1.   2.

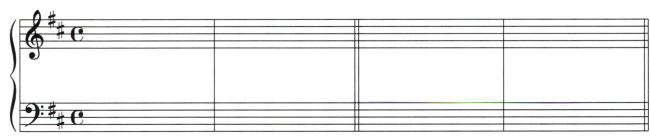

b:

3.

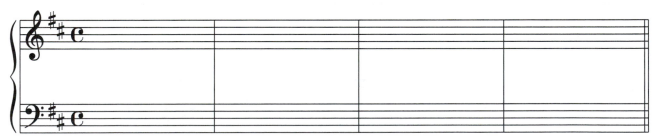

4.

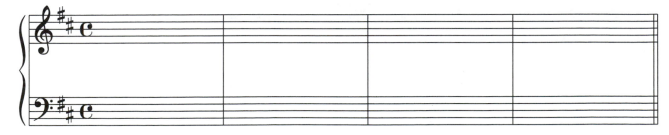

Phrase model 2

♭6   ♮

Expansion 1.

2.

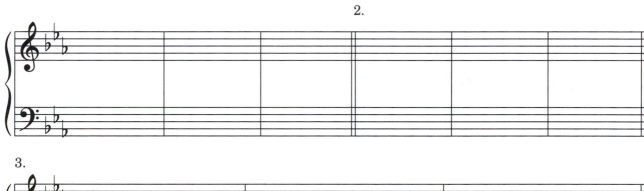

3.

4.

5.

6.

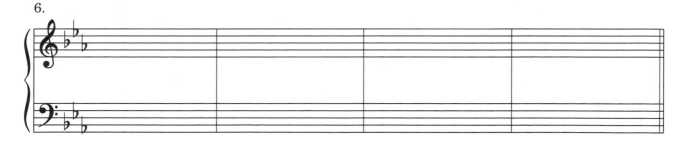

ANALYSIS

DVD 1
CH 29
TRACK 12

EXERCISE 29.26

Brahms, Waltz in E major, op. 39, no. 12
Answer questions that follow the score.

1. What is the form of this piece?
2. What is the overall tonal motion in the first part?
3.
    a. What important harmonic change occurs in mm. 13ff?
    b. Why do you think Brahms employs this harmonic technique? (Hint: where does it go?)
4. What harmony is expanded in mm. 16–20? What is unusual about the expansion? (Hint: What makes it unstable, and why would Brahms have written it this way?)

KEYBOARD

EXERCISE 29.27 Illustrations

Complete the illustrations in the order described.

A. In D minor: expand the tonic, include ♭II6, lead to V with an applied diminished seventh chord; close with a HC.

B. In A minor: use a D2 (–5/+4) sequence with alternating nondominant sevenths that leads to ♭II6; close with a PAC.

C. In F major: expand the tonic using a descending bass arpeggiation; tonicize iii using a ♭II6 in that key; close with a PAC in the key of iii.

D. In C major: establish the tonic; tonicize ♭III; move to a cadential six-four chord, close with a PAC.

E. In G minor: establish the tonic; tonicize III; include an A2 (–3/+4) sequence with applied chords that leads to VI; use ♭II6 as the pre-dominant; lead to V with a vii°7/V and close with a PAC.

F. In D major: establish the tonic; tonicize ♭VI; continue a descending arpeggiation to ♭II; close with a PAC in D major.

EXERCISE 29.28 Figured Bass

Realize the figured bass in four voices; analyze by using two levels. Not all suspensions may be able to be prepared. You may write in a few soprano pitches.

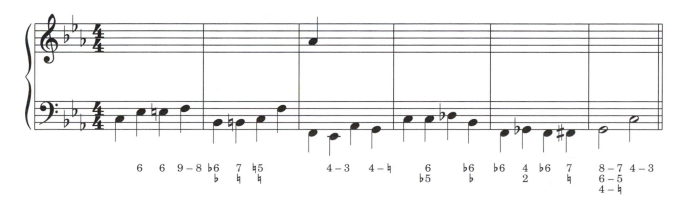

EXERCISE 29.29

Harmonize in four voices the following soprano melodies. Look for opportunities to incorporate the Neapolitan, mixture harmonies, and sequences. Analyze. Be able to play your progressions on the piano.

A.

B.

EXERCISE 29.30 Road Map

In D minor, complete the tasks below.

A. Establish the tonic, using any contrapuntal progression that includes a suspension.

B. Tonicize III; include a mixture chord in the tonicization.

C. Using an A2 (−3/+4) sequence with applied chords, move to VI (of D minor) and briefly tonicize that harmony.

D. Tonicize ♭II using at least four chords.

E. Using ♭II as a pivot, reinterpret it in the key of iv (of D minor), and close using a PAC in the new key of iv. Include a ♭II in the closing progression and at least two suspensions.

Optional: Orchestrate your progression for string quartet or piano and voice (in which case you must design an accompanimental texture).

CHAPTER 30

The Augmented Sixth Chord

Exercises for General Features of Augmented Sixth Chords: Types, Writing, Hearing

ASSIGNMENT 30.1

ANALYSIS

DVD 1
CH 30
TRACK 1

EXERCISE 30.1

Listen to and analyze the following "analytical snapshots," each of which contains an augmented sixth chord. Label the augmented sixth as follows: "It$_3^6$," "Ger$_5^6$," or "Fr$_3^4$."

A. Bach, "Ich hab' mein' Sach' Gott heimgestellt," BWV 351
   1. The pitch that creates the characteristic interval of the augmented sixth appears just after the other chord tones of the sonority. How does Bach postpone this pitch?
   2. Convert the ii°6 chord in m. 2 into a ♭II6 (Neapolitan) harmony.

B. Mozart, Piano Trio no. 7 in E♭ major, K. 498, *Allegretto*

C. Beethoven, *Finale:* Violin Sonata no. 7 in C Minor, op. 30, no. 2, *Allegro*
    One could argue that all three forms (a world tour) of the augmented sixth appear in this example. Label each form.

D. Mozart, Piano Concerto in E♭ major, K. 449, *Allegro*

WRITING

EXERCISE 30.2 Writing and Resolving Augmented Sixth Chords

We now generate the three forms of the augmented sixth chord from the phrygian cadence. Follow this procedure, noting the various chords on a separate sheet of manuscript paper.

1. Determine the minor key implied by key signature.
2. Write a phrygian cadence (i.e., iv6–V)
3. Transform the phrygian cadence into an It6 (raise $\hat{4}$).
4. Transform the It6 into a Ger$^6_5$ (add a fifth above the bass: $\hat{3}$) and resolve the chord to a cadential six-four chord.
5. Transform the Ger$^6_5$ into a Fr$^4_3$ (substitute an augmented fourth above the bass by lowering the fifth of the Ger$^6_5$ a semitone: $\hat{2}$).

Sample solution

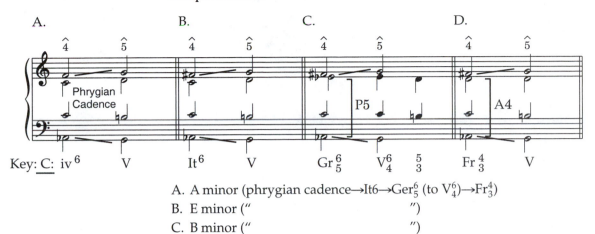

Key: C: iv⁶   V   It⁶   V   Gr⁶₅   V⁶₄ ⁵₃   Fr⁴₃   V

A. A minor (phrygian cadence→It6→Ger⁶₅ (to V⁶₄)→Fr⁴₃)
B. E minor ("   ")
C. B minor ("   ")

EXERCISE 30.3 Spelling Augmented Sixth Chords

Notate on a separate sheet of manuscript paper the following augmented sixth chords and resolve them to the dominant. Add necessary chromaticism; do not use key signatures.

G minor:	D major:	A major:	C♯ minor:	B minor:	B♭ major:
Fr⁴₃	It 6	Ger⁶₅	Fr⁴₃	Ger⁶₅	It 6

LISTENING

DVD 1
CH 30
TRACK 2

EXERCISE 30.4

Listen to the examples below and label the chord used as a pre-dominant; your choices are: iv, ii°6, ♭II6, or +6 (specify type of +6; remember that the It⁶₃ moves directly to V and the Ger⁶₅ moves to a cadential six-four).

A. ___ B. ___ C. ___ D. ___ E. ___ F. ___ G. ___ H. ___

I. ___ J. ___ K. ___ L. ___ M. ___ N. ___ O. ___

ASSIGNMENT 30.2

ANALYSIS

DVD 1
CH 30
TRACK 3

EXERCISE 30.5

Listen to and analyze the two examples below. Label augmented sixth chords fully (It$_3^6$, Ger$_5^6$, or Fr$_3^4$).

A. Schubert, Waltz in F major, *36 Originaltänze*, no. 34, D. 365

1. The dominant harmony in m. 3 might be viewed as a ninth chord since the D5 (a ninth above the bass) is not treated as a dissonance; that is, it is not a passing or neighboring tone or a suspension. Yet one can also view the ninth as resolving in m. 5, making it only an apparent chord tone. Which interpretation do you prefer?

2. What is the form of this piece? Hint: Is this a binary form or merely a period?

B. Mozart, String Quartet no. 15 in D minor, K. 421, *Allegro*

1. What type of bass line occurs twice in this example? What is the basic difference between the two appearances?
2. How would you explain the dissonant B♭ in violin I of m. 3?
3. How does Mozart prepare in the first phrase for the augmented sixth chord that appears in the second phrase?

B.

LISTENING

DVD 1
CH 30
TRACK 4

EXERCISE 30.6 Bass Line Notation of Augmented Sixth Chords

Notate the bass and analyze the following examples with pre-dominant harmonies that include the augmented sixth chord. Focus first on the underlying chord progression and the type of pre-dominant. One way to distinguish supertonic harmonies (including ♭II) from augmented sixth harmonies is that the bass of supertonic harmonies ascends to V but the bass of the augmented sixth descends to V. Thus, once you have determined the bass's motion, you need only distinguish between ii and ♭II.

A.

B.

C.

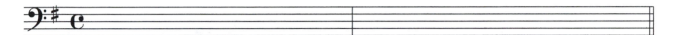

D.

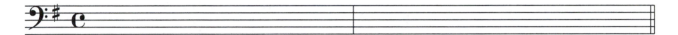

E.

EXERCISE 30.7 Motion to and from Augmented Sixth Chords

Determine and label the key in which each of the augmented sixth chords below occurs. Then do the following.

1. Precede each +6 with a root-position tonic chord.
2. Resolve each +6 chord to the dominant.

Sample solution

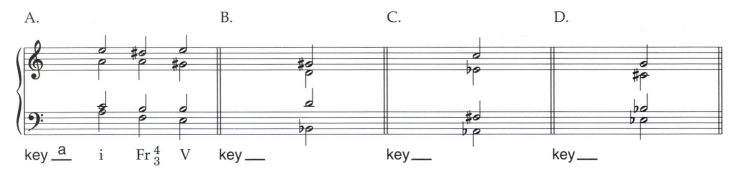

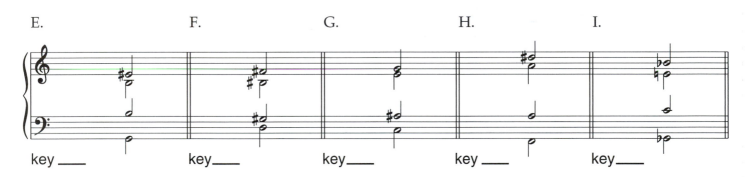

EXERCISE 30.8 Figured Bass

Realize the figured basses below in four voices and analyze.

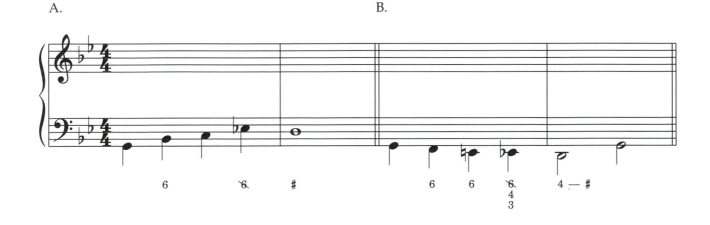

ASSIGNMENT 30.3

LISTENING

DVD 1
CH 30
TRACK 5

EXERCISE 30.9 Bass Line Notation of Augmented Sixth Chords

Notate the bass and analyze the following examples with pre-dominant harmonies that include the augmented sixth chord. Focus first on the underlying
chord progression and the type of pre-dominant.

A.

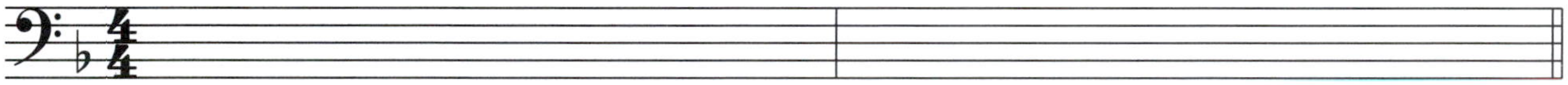

B.

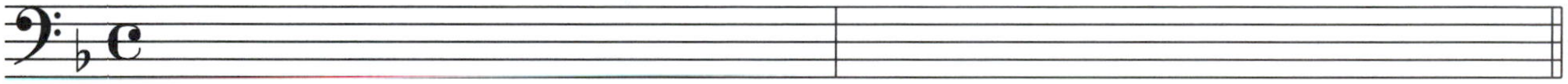

C.

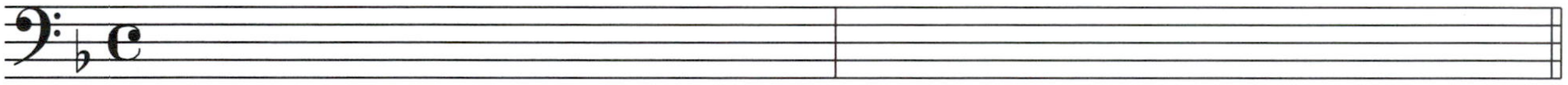

D.

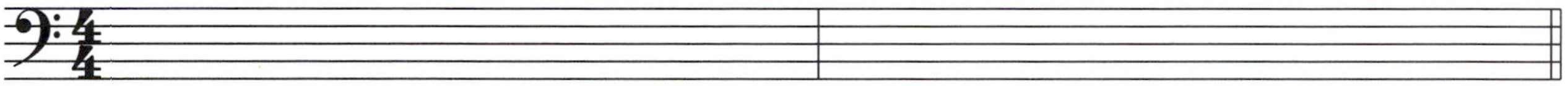

E.

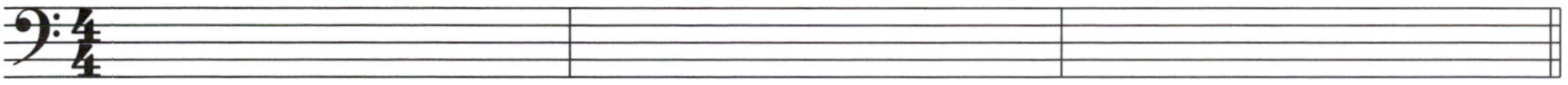

WRITING

EXERCISE 30.10 Figured Bass

Realize the figured bass below in four voices and analyze.

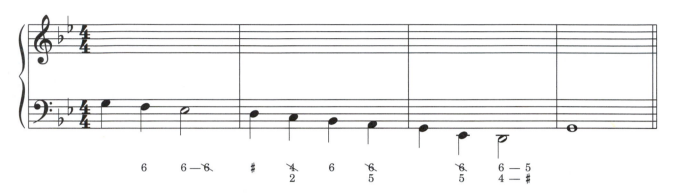

KEYBOARD

EXERCISE 30.11

Realize the two figured basses below, each of which contains a bass descent.

A.   B.

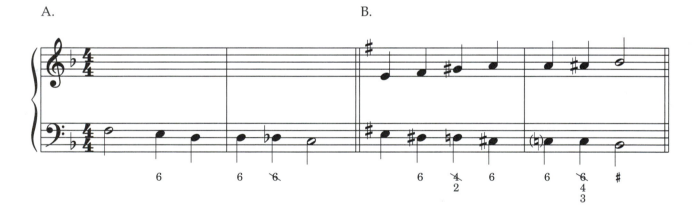

ANALYSIS

DVD 1
CH 30
TRACK 6

EXERCISE 30.12

Each of the three operatic excerpts below contains tonicizations of two or more keys, and each tonicization is signaled by an augmented sixth chord. Label each key, then analyze the pre-dominant–dominant motion.

A.   Verdi, "Qual voce come tu donna?" from *Il Trovatore*, part 4, no. 18

B.   Ponchielli, "Ombre di mia prosopia" from *La Gioconda*

(continues on next page)

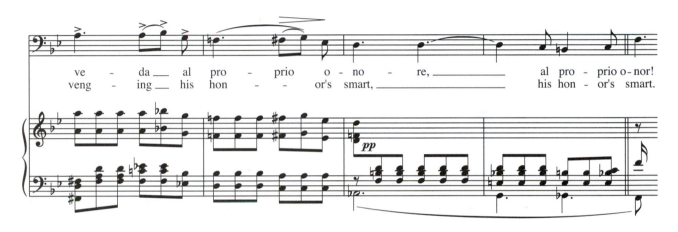

C. Verdi, "Dormiro sol" from *Don Carlo*

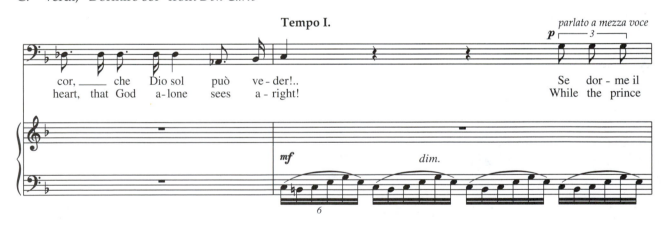

(continues on next page)

D. Wagner, "Mein Herr und Gott" from *Lohengrin*

ASSIGNMENT 30.4

ANALYSIS AND LISTENING

DVD 1
CH 30
TRACK 7

EXERCISE 30.13

The following excerpts include the upper voices. Notate the basses and include roman numerals.

A. Schubert, "Wehmut" ("Melancholy"), op. 22, no. 2, D. 772

B. "Lamento di Magdalena"

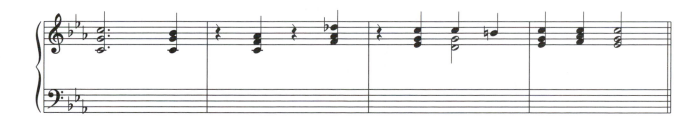

C.   Haydn, String Quartet in E♭ major, op. 76, no. 6, Hob. III:80, *Allegretto*

EXERCISE 30.14 Longer Dictation

Notate the bass and soprano of the four-measure examples and analyze. Exercises C and D modulate.

A.

B.

C.

D.

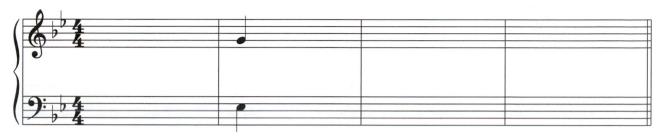

WRITING

EXERCISE 30.15 Short Illustrations

Complete the following tasks in four voices. Analyze.

A. In A minor, use any augmented sixth to harmonize the following soprano melody: $\hat{3}$–$\hat{4}$–$\sharp\hat{4}$–$\hat{5}$.

B. In E minor, write a progression that expands the tonic, includes a Fr^4_3, and closes with a HC.

C. In F major, write a progression that includes an It^6_3 chord and a suspension.

D. In D major, write a parallel interrupted period that contains two different types of + 6 chords.

A.

B.

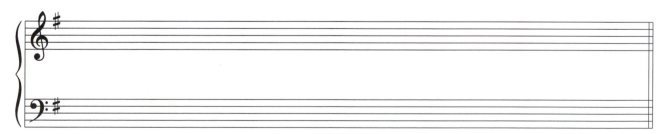

C.

D.

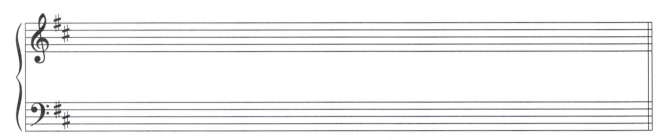

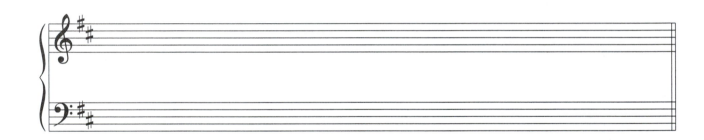

ASSIGNMENT 30.5

LISTENING

DVD 1
CH 30
TRACK 9

EXERCISE 30.16

The following excerpts include the upper voices. Notate the basses and include roman numerals.

A. Schubert, "Die Liebe hat gelogen" ("Love Has Lied"), op. 23, no. 1, D. 751

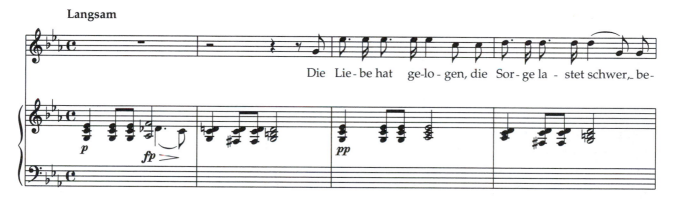

B. Gluck, "Sweet Affection, Heavenly Treasure," Trio from *Orpheus and Evrydice,* act III, no. 50

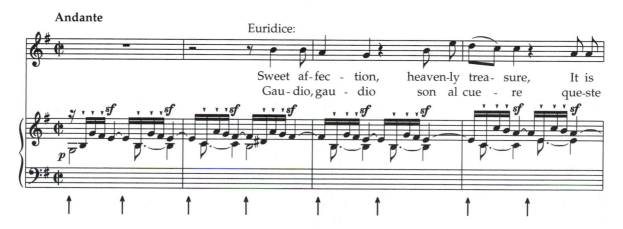

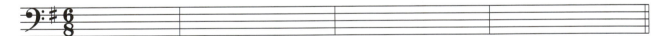

EXERCISE 30.17 Dictation of Figurated Examples

Notate the bass lines of each of the following phrases and analyze with roman begins with numerals.

A.   begins with upbeat

B.   **Allegretto**

C.   **Lento**

D. Haydn, String Quartet in B♭ major, op. 50, no. 1, Hob. III:44, *Adagio non lento*

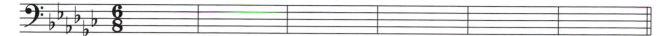

E. Gluck, "Sorrowing Mortal" from *Orpheus and Eurydice,* act I, no. 23

Lento

WRITING

EXERCISE 30.18 Melody Harmonization

Study the melodic fragments below and harmonize each in four voices according to the instructions. Analyze.

A. Include an It$^6_3$ and step-descent bass.

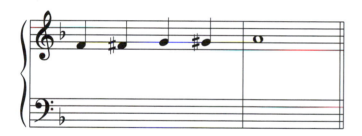

B. Include a Ger$^6_5$ and an applied chord.

C. Include a Fr$^4_3$ and deceptive cadence.

D. Include an applied chord and an augmented sixth chord.

Exercises for ♭VI and +6, +6 in Pre-Dominant Expansions, +6 and Modulation: Reinforcement and Pivot

ASSIGNMENT 30.6

LISTENING

EXERCISE 30.19 Dictation of Expanded ♭VI and Conversion to Augmented Sixth.

DVD 1
CH 30
TRACK 11

Notate the bass and soprano lines for each excerpt except the last one, where you may notate only the bass (do not notate repeated pitches). Analyze.

A.

B.

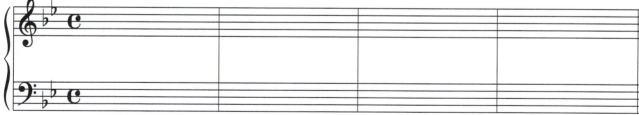

C.   notate upbeat

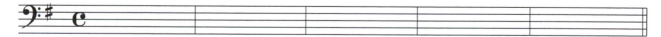

WRITING

EXERCISE 30.20 Figured Bass

Realize the figured bass below in four voices. Analyze.

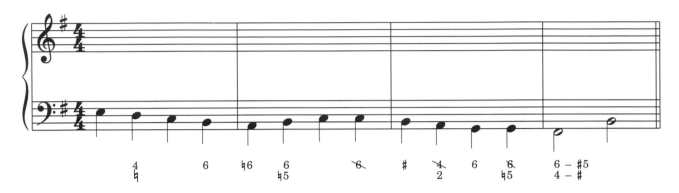

ANALYSIS

DVD 1
CH 30
TRACK 12

EXERCISE 30.21

Listen to the excerpts below, in which (♭)VI is converted into an +6 chord. Label the expanded submediant and circle and label the type of +6 chord. Answer any questions in a sentence or two.

A. Beethoven, Andante in F major, WoO 57
What sequential progression occurs in the excerpt's beginning? What harmony is prolonged in mm. 2–4?

(continues on next page)

B. Haydn, *Menuett*, String Quartet in C major, op. 74, no. 1, Hob:III.72.
    Identify the type of binary form. (You will be listening to the A section, the digression, and the three measures that immediately follow the digression). What type of sequence is used in the digression, and what harmony does it extend?

(continues on next page)

C. Schubert, Waltz in A major, *Wiener-Damen Ländler*, no. 6, D. 734
   What is the form of this piece?

ASSIGNMENT 30.7

LISTENING

EXERCISE 30.22 Dictation of Modulations Featuring the Augmented Sixth Chord

DVD 1
CH 30
TRACK 13

Each of the four modulating phrases contains a prominent augmented sixth chord. You are given the upper voices in the first two exercises: notate only the bass and analyze. Notate both soprano and bass for Exercises C and D. Analyze using two levels.

A.

B.

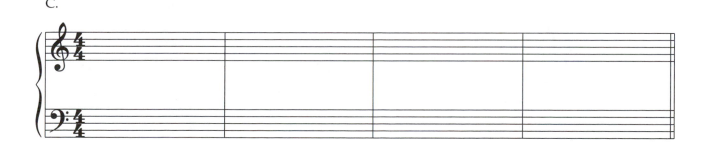

C.

D.

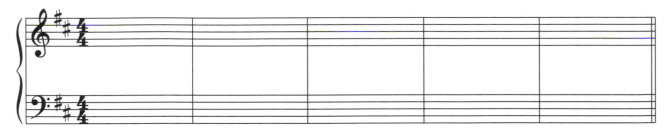

WRITING

EXERCISE 30.23 Illustrations

Complete the following tasks on a sheet of manuscript paper. Analyze.

A. In D major, move to ♭VI, and prolong it briefly through tonicization. Then, destabilize ♭VI by converting it into a Fr_3^4. Close with a PAC.

B. Modulate from F major to ♭III. Use an augmented sixth chord in each key.

C. Modulate from B minor to its VI. Use a chromatic step-descent bass in the original key. Employ any sequence in the new key and any augmented sixth chord.

ANALYSIS

DVD 1
CH 30
TRACK 14

EXERCISE 30.24 Expanded Pre-Dominants and Augmented Sixth–Diminished Third Chords

Analyze the excerpts that combine extended pre-dominants and augmented sixth chords. Circle the pre-dominant area; then analyze each sonority.

A.   Haydn, Piano Sonata in E major, Hob. XVI:31, *Allegretto*

B.   Beethoven, String Quartet no. 11 in F minor, "Serioso," op. 95, *Larghetto espressivo*

C.   Gluck, Ritornello from *Orpheus and Eurydice*, act I, no. 6

ASSIGNMENT 30.8

EXERCISE 30.25 Aural Examples from the Literature

Notate the bass for each of the examples below. Analyze.

A. Haydn, Piano Sonata no. 38 in F major, Hob. XVI:23, *Adagio*

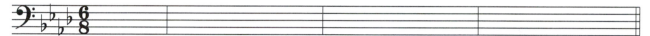

B. Beethoven, String Quartet no. 3 in D major, op. 18, no. 3, *Minore*

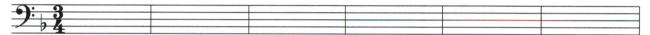

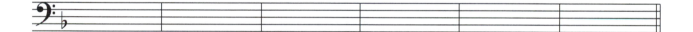

C. Gluck, "His Moving Elegies" from *Orpheus and Eurydice*, act II, no. 27
This example begins on V. What harmony is prolonged over this example?

EXERCISE 30.26 Analysis of Enharmonic Modulations Using the Augmented Sixth Chord

Identify the point at which the augmented sixth chord is transformed enharmonically into a dominant in the following musical excerpts. No roman numeral analysis is necessary. Even though you will hear tonicizations, not "modulations," use the pivot chord labeling technique:

Sample solution

I: $\boxed{\text{Ger}_5^6}$

♭II: $\boxed{\text{V7}}$

A.

B.

C.   Beethoven, Piano Sonata no. 27 in E major, op. 90, *Nicht zu geschwind und sehr singbar vorzutragen*

D.   Schubert, Piano Sonata in A minor, op. 42, D. 845, *Moderato*

E.   Schubert, *Originaltänze*, op. 9, no. 14, D. 365

(continues on next page)

WRITING

EXERCISE 30.27 Composition

Choose one of the following antecedent phrases given and then write a consequent phrase to create a parallel progressive period. Incorporate one example of ♭II and an augmented sixth chord. Analyze. In Example C, transform the 4-measure chord progression into a 12-measure composition by slowing the harmonic rhythm. This is easiest if you develop a motivic idea and create an accompanimental pattern from the homophonic chord progression. Consider appropriate metrical placement for the harmonies.

Additional Exercises

LISTENING

DVD 1
CH 30
TRACK 17

EXERCISE 30.28 Dictation

The following progressions contain expanded pre-dominants and enharmonic reinterpetation of +6 chords. Notate bass and soprano; analyze. Possible expansions are as follows:

- iv→P$_4^6$→iv6
- iv6→P$_4^6$→ii°6
- iv→P$_4^6$→+6
- Ger$_5^6$→P$_4^6$→Ger°7
- iv6→P$_4^6$→$^\flat$II^6

A.

B.

C.

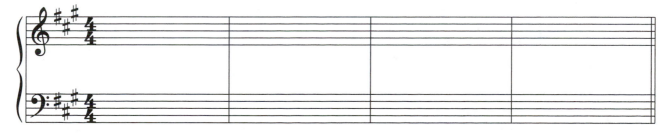

D.

EXERCISE 30.29 Aural Examples from the Literature

Notate the bass and provide roman numerals for each of the examples below.

A.   Haydn, Piano Sonata in D major, Hob. XVI:33, *Adagio*

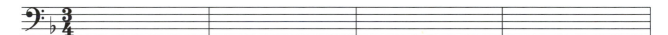

B.   Schubert, Waltz in C minor, *Wiener Deutsche*, no. 6, D. 128
This example is slightly longer (12 mm.), but the bass line should be easy to follow. What is the chromatic pre-dominant chord that leads to the final cadence?

Allegro molto

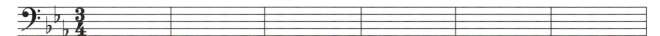

C.   Schumann, Waltz in A minor, *Albumblätter,* op. 124, no. 6

Allegro

EXERCISE 30.30 Two-Voice Dictation

Notate the florid two-voice counterpoint. Include a harmonic analysis.

A.

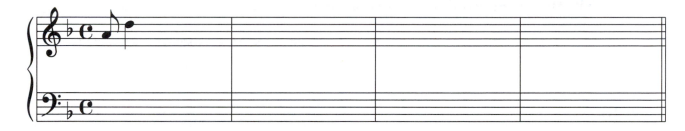

B.

C.

WRITING

EXERCISE 30.31 Brain Teaser

Consider the following two harmonies: C–E–G–B♭ and C–E–G–A♯.
Determine the key in which these function as a dominant seventh and a German sixth, respectively. Then, write a progression that demonstrates each chord's behavior.

EXERCISE 30.32 Writing the Diminished Third Chord

Write the following chords and resolve them to the dominant:
A. Ger 7 in C minor   B. Ger$_5^6$ in D minor   C. Ger 7 in C# minor
D. Ger$_5^6$—P$_4^6$—Ger 7 in A minor E. Ger$_5^6$—Ger°3 with voice exchange in G minor

EXERCISE 30.33 Figured and Unfigured Basses

Realize the following figured and unfigured basses. Include a harmonic analysis.

WRITING

EXERCISE 30.34

Complete the following passage in four-voice chorale style. You are given the following:

mm. 1–2: unfigured bass   mm. 3–4: melody harmonization

mm. 5–6: figured bass   mm. 7–8: figured bass + melody

Add the remaining voices and analyze. Include one of each type of augmented sixth chord.

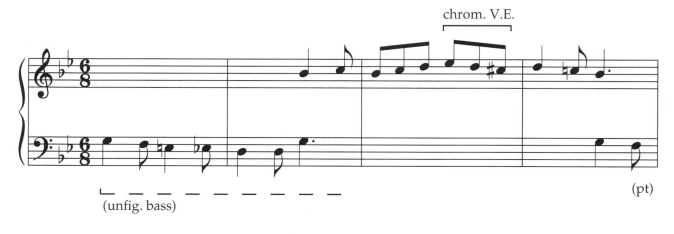

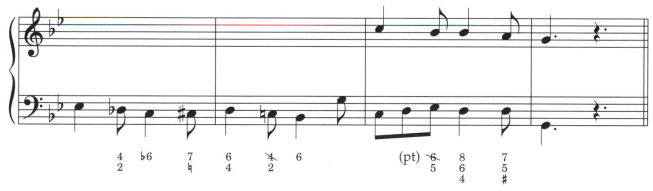

KEYBOARD

EXERCISE 30.35 Review

The unfigured bass and soprano below contains sequences, applied chords, modulations, mixture, and the Neapolitan. Play in four voices and analyze using two levels.

(continues on next page)

EXERCISE 30.36 Figured Bass

Add the inner voices to the given soprano, bass and figures. Analyze using two levels. Be able to sing the bass while you play the other voices.

A.   B.

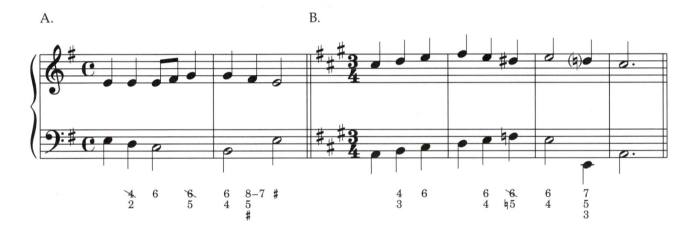

C.

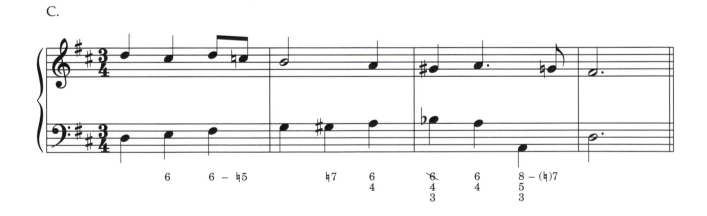

EXERCISE 30.37 Road Map

Below is a musical outline that includes instructions for your composition and the length of each section. Analyze.

| establish tonic contrapuntally | move to ♭VI through passing V$^4_3$/♭VI | establish ♭VI harmonically for 2 – 3 mm. End up on V^7/♭VI. Treat it as a Ger $^6_5$ and resolve to V–I in new key. |

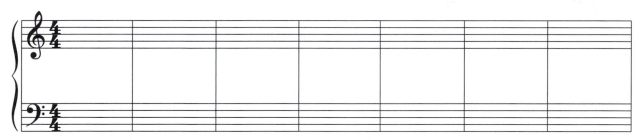

| begin A2(–3/+4) +app$^6_5$; treat arrival as minor tonic | use D2(–5/+4) to mod. to III of this key. | expand +6 with V in this new key; end w/PAC. What key is this? |

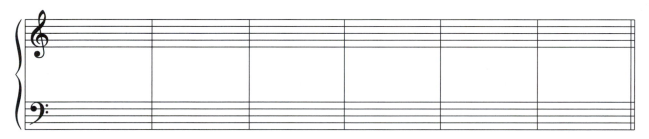

ANALYSIS

DVD 1
CH 30
TRACK 20

EXERCISE 30.38

Analyze the following examples using roman numerals.

A.   Mozart, Piano Trio in G major, K. 564, *Andante*

(continues on next page)

B.   Chopin, Mazurka in C♯ minor, op. 63, no. 3

C.   Leopold Mozart, from Trio Sonata in E♭ major, op. 1, no. 2, *Andante*

D.

E.

F.

G.

H.

I.

J.

K.

L.

M.

N.

O.

CHAPTER 31

Ternary Form

ASSIGNMENT 31.1

ANALYSIS

DVD 1
CH 31
TRACK 1

EXERCISE 31.1 Ternary and Binary Forms

Recall that there may be some ambiguity between a work cast in ternary form with transitions and retransitions and one that is written in rounded binary form. To compare and contrast these forms, study the example below. Could this example be viewed as being either binary or ternary? Listen to and study the piece to develop an interpretation. Then, make a formal diagram that includes the major sections, transitions, and retransitions. Finally, summarize your interpretation in a paragraph.

Haydn, Trio, Piano Sonata in D major, Hob. XVI:14

Label any sequences and discuss in a sentence or two their function within the passage.

ANALYSIS AND DICTATION

DVD 1
CH 31
TRACK 2

EXERCISE 31.2

This exercise is identical to Exercise 31.1 except that the bass line is omitted from areas of the example. Notate the missing bass notes by listening and by the implications of the given upper voices. Further, analyze the piece in its entirety. In addition, provide a complete formal label that includes subsections and accompanying harmonic areas. In a sentence or two, support your choice of form with relevant examples. Finally, answer the accompanying questions.

Schumann, "Albumblätter, I," *Bunte Blätter*, op. 99

Brahms later used this small piece as the theme for a set of variations for piano solo. What type of phrase–period structure occurs in mm. 1–8 and 17–24?

LISTENING

EXERCISE 31.3 Aural Identification and Analysis of Ternary and Binary Forms

DVD 1
CH 31
TRACK 3

We turn now to listening to and answering questions about ternary and binary forms without the aid of the score. Provide a formal diagram and formal label for each piece. Include a phrase–period diagram for the first two phrases. Support your answers carefully in a short paragraph.

Beethoven, Bagatelle no. 11 in A major, op 119, no. 4

ASSIGNMENT 31.2

ANALYSIS

EXERCISE 31.4 Ternary and Binary Form

Could this example be viewed as being either binary or ternary? Listen to and
study the piece carefully to develop an interpretation. Then, make a formal diagram that includes the major sections, transitions, and retransitions. Answer the
leading questions that accompany the example. Finally, summarize your interpretation in a paragraph.

Chopin, Mazurka in E minor, op. 17, no. 2, BI 77

(continues on next page)

(continues on next page)

1. Discuss examples of the important role that unprepared dissonance plays in this piece.
2. Discuss the phrase–period structure in mm. 1–12 and in mm. 1–24.
3. What is the underlying harmonic motion in mm. 1–12?
4. The material in mm. 25ff contrasts with the material in the first section. One could argue, however, that many of the melodic gestures could be traced back to the first section. Support this assertion with examples; in particular, focus on the opening tune of the *Dolce* section and the chromatic material over the G pedal that follows.

ANALYSIS AND DICTATION

DVD 1
CH 31
TRACK 5

EXERCISE 31.5

The bass line is omitted from areas of this example. Notate the missing bass notes by listening and by the implications of the given upper voices. Further, analyze the piece in its entirety and provide a complete formal label that includes subsections and accompanying harmonic areas. In a sentence or two, support your choice of form with relevant examples.

Mozart, *Menuetto*, Serenade in D major for Strings and Winds, "Haffner", K. 250

(continues on next page)

LISTENING

EXERCISE 31.6 Aural Identification and Analysis of Ternary and Binary Forms

We now return to listening to and answering questions about ternary and binary forms without the aid of a score. Provide a formal diagram and formal label for the piece. Include subsections in your diagram.

Schumann, "Sizilianisch," *Album für die Jugend*, op. 68, no. 11

Cast in $\frac{6}{8}$ and a fairly rapid tempo, this piece begins in A minor. In what key are we in m. 8?

ASSIGNMENT 31.3

ANALYSIS

EXERCISE 31.7 Ternary and Binary Forms

Study the piece to be able to develop an interpretation. Then, make a formal diagram that includes the major sections, transitions, and retransitions. Answer the leading questions that accompany the example. Finally, summarize your interpretation in a paragraph.

Beethoven, Bagatelle No. 8 in G minor, op. 119, no. 1

(continues on next page)

1. How many phrases occur in mm. 1–16? Do they combine to form one or more periods?
2. There is an interesting relationship between mm. 1–4 and mm. 5–8. Discuss. Hint: Study the relationship between the hands.
3. Given the prominence of the upper-neighbor figure, $\hat{5}$–$\hat{6}$–$\hat{5}$, might this be viewed as a motive? Trace other statements of this figure—both on the surface and below the surface (i.e., migration to the bass and harmonic structure)— and/or any other motivic ideas that you may find interesting.

ANALYSIS/DICTATION

EXERCISE 31.8

The bass line is omitted from areas of this example. Notate the missing bass notes (arrows) by listening and by the implications of the given upper voices. Analyze the piece in its entirety and provide a complete formal label that includes subsections and accompanying harmonic areas. In a sentence or two, support your choice of form with relevant examples.

Brahms, Waltz in E minor, *Waltzes for Piano*, op. 39, no. 4
What type of phrase structure occurs in mm. 1–8?

(continues on next page)

ASSIGNMENT 31.4

ANALYSIS

DVD 1
CH 31
TRACK 9

EXERCISE 31.9 Ternary and Binary Forms

Listen to and study the piece carefully, to be able to develop an interpretation. Then, make a formal diagram that includes the major sections, transitions, and re-transitions. Answer the leading questions that accompany the example. Finally, summarize your interpretation in a paragraph.

Haydn, *Menuetto:* String Quartet in F major, op. 74, no. 2, Hob. III:73, *Allegro*

(continues on next page)

(continues on next page)

1. Provide a two-level harmonic analysis that details (a) the deepest-level tonal relations of the movement and (b) tonicizations within formal sections.
2. What type of period opens the movement? How many phrases are there? How are they linked harmonically?
3. The chromaticism that appears in m. 4 is striking, almost shocking. Haydn often injects chromaticism into the opening of a piece, and, as we have seen in the work of other composers, the chromaticism appears throughout the movement and may be often developed in ways that help explain unusual tonal relations as simply harmonizations, and thus stabilizations, of chromatic pitches. Explore the reappearance of such chromaticism.
4. What is the function of the material in mm. 28–41? What would be a good label for this section?
5. Label and discuss the tonal functions of sequential passages.

LISTENING

EXERCISE 31.10 Aural Identification and Analysis of Ternary and Binary Forms

We now listen to and answer some more questions about ternary and binary forms without the aid of a score. Provide a formal diagram and formal label. Include subsections in your diagram. Support your answers carefully in a short paragraph.

Schumann, "Winterzeit I," *Album für die Jugend,* op. 68, no. 38

Below is an incomplete score for mm. 1–5. Notate the missing bass line.

CHAPTER 32

Rondo

ASSIGNMENT 32.1

ANALYSIS

DVD 1
CH 32
TRACK 1

EXERCISE 32.1

Listen to and study the score, make a form diagram, and answer the following questions.

Haydn, Finale, Piano Sonata no. 50 in D major, Hob. XVI: 37, *Presto, ma non troppo*

(continues on next page)

(continues on next page)

1. The sectional character of this rondo is enhanced by nested forms that are either ternary or binary types. Label the specific type of these nested forms.
2. Discuss any changes that occur in the restatements of the refrain.
3. One could view the material that begins in m. 28 as derived from earlier material. Explore this possibility.

AURAL ANALYSIS

EXERCISE 32.2

You will hear a rondo, for which no score is included. Answer the following questions and complete the tasks:

Beethoven, Piano Sonata no. 9 in E major, op. 14, no. 1, *Allegro comodo*

1. There is a transition between the refrain and the first episode; from what material is it derived?
2. There is a transition that moves to the C section. What crucial harmonic change occurs at the beginning of the transition, and how does it help prepare the key of G major?
3. The key of the C section is G major. Is this unusual, and if so, why?
4. What rhythmic effect occurs in the final statement of the refrain?
5. Make a formal diagram that includes the prevailing key of each section. Make sure that you have answered the preceding questions, since they will guide your listening.

ASSIGNMENT 32.2

ANALYSIS

EXERCISE 32.3 Analysis

Handel, "Vaghe pupille" ("O Lovely Eyes") from *Orlando*, HWV 31, act 2, scene 9
Rondos appear in a variety of genres, including opera. The piece below is an aria
cast in rondo form.

1. Make a formal diagram that includes section labels and key structure. Make
   sure that you show transitions and retransitions and include measure
   numbers.
2. Discuss how the highly contrasting sections are demarcated
3. What is the recurring harmonic pattern called that appears throughout one
   of the episodes?
4. The material that occurs in m. 108 is interrupted by a section marked *tutti*.
   What musical role does this interruption play?

(continues on next page)

va - ghe pu - pil - le, nò, non pian-ge - te _ nò, nò, _____ non pian-ge-te, nò, nò, _____ non pian-ge-te, nò,

Larghetto

Viol. piano, senza Oboe.

che del pian - to an-cor nel re - gno può in ogn' un de - star _____ pie - tà, può

de-star _____ de-star pie - tà, che del

(continues on next page)

(continues on next page)

no pian-ge-te,   nò,   nò, ____ non pian-ge-te, no!   Ma   sì,   sì,   sì, pu-pil-le,__ sì,   sì,   sì, pian-ge-te,__

sì,   che sor-do al vo stro in-can - to,   che   sor-do al vo stro in-can -   -   -   -

- to   ho un co - re   d'a - da - man - - - to,   nè cal-ma il mio fu -

(continues on next page)

sì, pian - ge - te,   sì, pian - ge - te,   sì.

Si getta furiosamente dentro alla grotta che scoppia, vedendosi il mago
nel suo carro, che tiene frà le braccia Orlando, e fugge per aria.

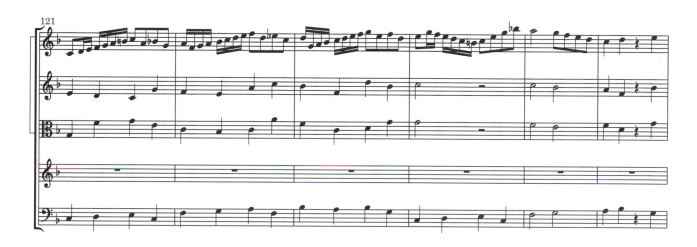

ASSIGNMENT 32.3

LISTENING

EXERCISE 32.4 Aural Analysis

You will hear a rondo, for which no score is included. Answer the following questions and complete the tasks:
Beethoven, Piano Sonata no. 8 in C minor, "Pathétique," op. 13, *Allegro*

1. Notate mm. 1–8 of the soprano tune of the refrain.

2. Discuss the tonal and phrase/formal structure of the refrain. Consider modulations, sequences, and unusual phrase characteristics.
3. The B section is in a major key. Based on your knowledge of rondo form, suggest Beethoven's most likely tonal possibility or possibilities.
4. What harmonic procedure occurs in the B section?
5. Below are the upper voices for a passage within the B section. Notate the missing bass voice and provide roman numerals (mm. 43–52).

6. Are there significant changes in repetitions of the refrain? Describe.
7. In what key is the C section? What contrapuntal technique characterizes this section?
8. Is this a five- or seven-part rondo? If seven, what changes occur in the repetition of the B section?
9. The closing measures of the movement are reproduced below. What formal label might you apply to this section? Provide roman numerals for these measures. Why might Beethoven have briefly tonicized the key that he does in mm. 200–206?

ASSIGNMENT 32.4

AURAL ANALYSIS

EXERCISE 32.5

A small portion of the score of a rondo you will hear is presented below. Answer the following questions and complete the tasks.

Beethoven, Violin Sonata no. 1 in D major, op. 12, no. 1, *Allegro*

1. Make a detailed formal chart of this movement that includes the key structure.
2. Below are the upper parts of the refrain. Listen to them, notate the bass, and provide roman numerals. What kind of period is this?

3. Which formal section is represented below? Notate the bass of the following four measures.

4. What important harmonic change takes place soon after the beginning of the second statement of the refrain? Be specific.
5. This change sets up the opening key of the C section. What is this key?
6. Below is an incomplete excerpt from near the end of the movement (the bass line is missing). What formal section does this immediately follow? How is the musical material deployed between the violin and the piano in this excerpt? What is this technique called?
7. Fill in the missing bass notes and provide roman numerals for the entire excerpt. Be aware that there is an important harmonic change that occurs in the bass line descent; the initial statement is labeled X and the altered statement is labeled Y. What exactly is changed?
8. What effect does this change at Y and the following measures have on the harmonic structure?

(continues on next page)

(continues on next page)

ASSIGNMENT 32.5

EXERCISE 32.6 Potpourri of Aural Analysis of Binary, Rondo, and Ternary Forms

DVD 1
CH 32
TRACK 2

You will hear three movements; no scores are included except for excerpts that accompany specific questions. Answer the following questions.

A. Haydn, *Finale*, Piano Sonata in D major, Hob. XVI: 19

1. Make a formal diagram that includes important key areas.
2. Do recurrences of material remain the same or change?

B. Haydn, *Menuetto*, String Quartet in G minor, op. 20, no. 3, Hob. III: 33, *Allegro*

1. Make a formal diagram that includes important keys.
2. Below is the incomplete score of mm 1–10. Notate the bass, give roman numerals, and then make a phrase-period diagram.

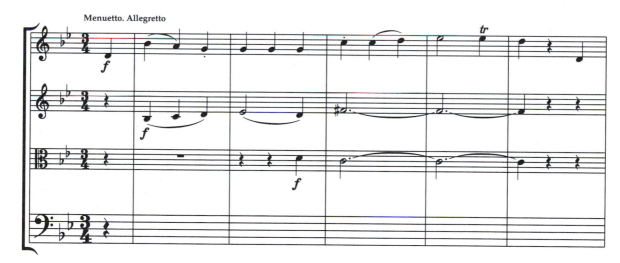

3. What contrapuntal device does Haydn employ later in this large section?
4. Below is the music that occurs near the close of the first large section. Notate the bass and provide roman numerals.

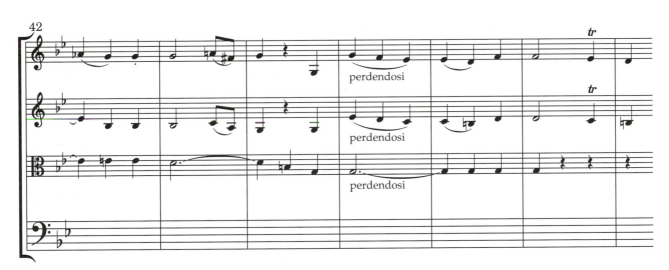

5. Below is the music that occurs near the end of another formal section. Notate the bass. What is the harmonic technique in this excerpt?

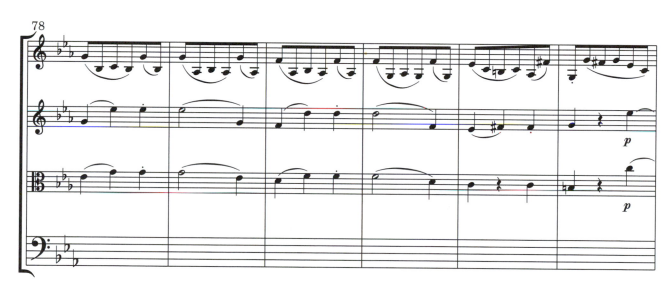

ASSIGNMENT 32.6

ANALYSIS

EXERCISE 32.7 Potpourri of Aural Analysis of Binary, Rondo and Ternary Forms

DVD 1
CH 32
TRACK 3

You will hear two movements; no scores are included. Answer the following questions.

A. Schumann, *Kreisleriana*, op. 16, no. 3

1. Make a detailed formal diagram that includes the form and keys of any subsections.
2. What harmonic technique occurs in the opening section of the piece?

B. Mozart, Sonata no. 3 in A major for Flute and Piano, K. 12, *Allegro*

1. Make a formal diagram.
2. Make a phrase–period diagram of the opening period (the meter is $\frac{3}{8}$, felt as one beat per measure).
3. The material that follows the opening period is closely related to the opening material, yet is deployed differently; discuss.

ASSIGNMENT 32.7

ANALYSIS AND LISTENING

EXERCISE 32.8

DVD 1
CH 32
TRACK 4

You will hear two movements; no scores are included, except for an excerpt that accompanies specific questions for the Beethoven. Answer the following questions.

A. Schubert, String Quartet no. 11 in E major, op. 125, no. 2, D. 353, *Allegro vivace*

1. Make a formal diagram.
2. Make a phrase–period diagram for mm. 1–12. Discuss unusual features.
3. What chromatic harmony is tonicized in the following section? Hint: compare the opening sonority of that section with the end of the preceding section; focus on the motion in the cello part.

B. Beethoven, Piano Sonata no. 3 in C major, op. 2, no. 3, *Allegro assai*

1. Make a formal diagram that includes important keys.
2. Do mm. 1–8 form a period? Support your answer.
3. Below is the incomplete score from the opening of which formal section? Notate the bass line and provide roman numerals.

Additional Exercises

EXERCISE 32.9 Composition: Review of Periods and Chromatic Harmony

A. Write two consequent phrases to the given antecedent. The result will be a double period. The first consequent should close on V. After the given antecedent has been repeated, the second consequent should close in the tonic. Then, write a solo melody that will be performed above your homophonic accompaniment. Analyze.

B. Complete the excerpt below, which is in nineteenth-century mazurka style, by:

1. realizing the remaining figured bass for the eight-measure phrase
2. continuing the melody that was started
3. writing an appropriate eight-measure consequent phrase to create a PIP
4. analyzing each harmony and providing a second-level analysis

CHAPTER 33

Sonata Form

ASSIGNMENT 33.1

ANALYSIS

EXERCISE 33.1

Below is a movement cast in sonata form. Listen to the piece, then make a formal diagram that includes the location, name, and key of each section. Finally, answer the series of questions that follows.

Beethoven, Piano Sonata no. 1 in F minor, op. 2, no. 1, *Allegro*

1. Although this is Beethoven's first piano sonata with an opus (he wrote several earlier sonatas while in Bonn), it has many unusual events. For example, the first tonal area can be viewed as being exceptionally short, while the beginning of the second tonal area might be considered to balance the short FTA by its considerable length. Discuss these and other unusual features of this sonata.
2. Beethoven builds remarkable energy in mm. 1–8. Discuss how he accomplishes this by focusing on harmonic rhythm.
3. The E natural is left conspicuously hanging in m. 8. Some composers, including Beethoven, created connections between phrases and even sections of a work by endowing specific pitches with associative power. Explore this possibility in this movement, beginning with the $E\natural^5$ in m. 8.
4. What type of sequence appears in the transition? Where is the first authentic cadence in the STA? Is this unusual?
5. There are several sequences in the development. Label each.
6. One might view most of the development to lie in the key of $A\flat$ (III). Given this, list any keys that Beethoven tonicizes in relation to $A\flat$. Does $A\flat$ lead directly to the retransition, or is there another key that links $A\flat$ and the retransition's dominant?
7. This sonata illustrates how an initial surface motive can control almost all of the movement's subsequent melodic and harmonic material. Below is a reduction of mm. 1–8.

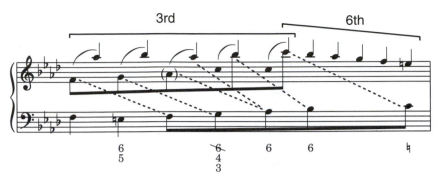

The opening ascending arpeggiation in the right hand moves to A♭5, followed by a turn figure around F. It is repeated a step higher and moves to B♭, followed by a turn around G. Both A♭5 (m. 5) and the B♭5 (m. 6) are marked *sforzando* and ascend to the C (m. 7), which is marked *fortissimo*. This ascent to C is balanced by a descent of a sixth from C⁶ to the hanging E♭⁵.

The bass voice exhibits a melodic pattern in mm. 1–8. The F³ is prolonged by its lower neighbor, E♮³, before it rises to C⁴ by stepwise motion. In fact, this same fifth ascent is manifested in the upper voice, by the F⁴ (m. 1) moving to G⁴ (m. 3), to A♭⁴ (m. 5), to B♭⁴ (m. 6), and finally to C⁵ (m. 7). We can now understand that by delaying the ascent in the bass for one measure, the neighboring V$^6_5$, (m. 3) transforms what would have been parallel octaves, resulting from the fifth ascent between the two voices, into a canon between the two voices.

Might this motivic sixth from the FTA also occur in other formal sections of the sonata? You may wish to look not only at the surface of thematic events, but also at any lines that occur below the surface, such as between the beginning and ending points of sequences. You could even explore the development for the opening motive's deep level repetition, a feature that we also saw in Mozart's B♭ major sonata K.333, which was discussed in the text. Do not ignore rhythmic correspondences.

ASSIGNMENT 33.2

ANALYSIS/DICTATION

DVD 1
CH 33
TRACK 1

EXERCISE 33.2

This exercise requires you to perform the same tasks as in Exercise 33.1. In addition, there are a few "bare spots" in the music, areas where the bass line is missing. Notate the bass line for these areas, marked with brackets.

Mozart, Piano Sonata in F major, K. 332, *Allegro*

1. What key is implied in addition to F major which is explicit in the movement's first phrase?
2. What contrapuntal and metric techniques occur in mm. 5–9?
3. What key is implied at the beginning of the transition? What about at the end of the transition? What key actually occurs at the STA?
4. What harmonic technique occurs in mm. 60–65? (Identification of this technique will aid in notating the missing bass line.)
5. What is the motivic relationship between the FTA theme and the theme in mm. 86–88?
6. Explore thematic/motivic relationships between mm. 89–93 and the opening two measures of the development.
7. What key is strongly implied in mm. 118–126? Is this key ever realized?
8. Does anything unusual occur in the FTA and the STA of the recapitulation? If so, describe.

(continues on next page)

ASSIGNMENT 33.3

DVD 1
CH 33
TRACK 2

EXERCISE 33.3

This exercise requires you to perform the same tasks as in Exercise 33.1. In addition, there are a few "bare spots" in the music, areas where the bass line is missing. Notate the bass line for these areas, marked with brackets and answer the questions that follow the score.

Mozart, Clarinet Quintet in A major, K. 581, *Allegro*
Note: Clarinet in A sounds a minor third lower than written.

1. The FTA begins with the strings and the clarinet almost at odds. That is, the strings are a unified group that presents the initial tunes, while the clarinet seems to play a subordinate role, only commenting on the strings' material, rather than presenting thematic material. Do you think that the strings play a more primary role throughout the movement, or does the clarinet begin to gain importance at some point? Develop the idea of a possible conflict in the interaction between strings and the clarinet.

2. A glance at the opening string gestures reveals a highly contrapuntal texture governed by contrary motion. In fact, the end points of the opening con-

trary-motion gestures (mm. 2 and 4) are on $\hat{6}$ (vi), creating the effect that the submediant harmony is preventing typical closure on the tonic (i.e., $\hat{5}$ moves to $\hat{6}$, rather than to $\hat{1}$). It is only in the third attempt to cadence that Mozart succeeds in an authentic cadence (m. 7), though the clarinet enters at that moment, weakening the tonic arrival by creating a phrase overlap. Explore the specific idea that various forms of deceptive motions stemming from $\hat{5}$ –$\hat{6}$ create drama throughout this movement. You may wish to discuss the more general 5–6 neighbor motion that also seems to play an important role both melodically and harmonically. Summarize your results in a paragraph or two, supporting your view with specific examples.

3. Bracket and label all sequential motions in the movement. Does one sequence type occur more often than the others? If so, can you trace the melodic motion of the sequence to the opening motivic gestures that were discussed in question 2?

4. Modal mixture is arguably the most important chromatic technique used in this movement. Identify at least four instances of mixture, making sure to include both local (surface) statements and deeper-level (tonal) statements. What contrapuntal technique generates many of these instances of mixture?

ASSIGNMENT 33.4

AURAL ANALYSIS

EXERCISE 33.4

You will hear a sonata movement with no score provided. Answer the series of questions similar to those above that accompany each movement.
Mozart, Piano Sonata in A minor, K. 310, *Allegro maestoso*

Exposition

1. What type of sequence is implied in the FTA?
2. Name the type of transition. Near the end of the transition, what unusual key is implied? (Be specific.)
3. In what key is the STA? Is this a monothematic sonata?
4. Is there a closing section? If so, how many subsections occur within the closing section?

Development

5. What key opens the development? What thematic material is used in this section?
6. The development comprises two giant sequences. What types are they. (Be careful, the first sequence is quite spread out.)
7. What harmony immediately precedes the V of the retransition and continues to expand V within the retransition?

Recapitulation

8. Compare the opening of the transition in the recapitulation to the opening of the transition in the exposition. Describe the difference in texture between these two places.
9. In what key is the STA of the recapitulation?
10. If there is a closing section in the recapitulation, compare it to the exposition: Are there any significant changes in the recapitulation's closing section (other than the obvious transposition to the tonic)?

ASSIGNMENT 33.5

AURAL ANALYSIS

DVD 1
CH 33
TRACK 3

EXERCISE 33.5

You will hear a sonata movement with no score provided. There are two types of tasks in this exercise. First, you must answer a series of questions similar to those above that will accompany each movement. The second task is new, and involves identifying formal sections and their keys. As you listen to the movement your teacher will call out numbers that represent points in the formal structure. You should answer the questions that correspond to these numbers. In general, you will be asked "Where are we in the form?" and you will respond with an answer such as "STA." There may be additional questions.

Haydn, String Quartet in G minor, "Horseman," op. 74, no. 3, Hob. III:74, *Allegro*
Answer the following questions based on the number called out

1. Where are we in the form?
2. What rhythmic effect is taking place here?
3. Where are we in the form and in what key?
4. Where are we in the form?
5. What harmonic progression is this?
6. What harmonic progression is this?
7. Where are we in the form? Is there anything unusual about it? If so, how would this impact the way you would analyze the opening of the movement?
8. Where are we in the form, and in what key?

Short-answer questions

1. The opening eight-measure "gallop" has a three-chord harmonic progression; use roman numerals to represent the chords.
2. What contrapuntal technique does Haydn use in the next phrase?
3. Comparing the harmonic content of these two phrases, what strikes you as very similar?
4. Is there a closing section in the exposition?
5. In what key does the exposition close?
6. In what key does the development begin? How long does this key last?
7. What thematic material is used in the development?
8. Discuss at least one unusual feature that occurs near the close of the development.
9. Are there significant differences between the exposition's transition and that which occurs in the recap? If so, what are they?

ASSIGNMENT 33.6

AURAL ANALYSIS

EXERCISE 33.6

You will hear a sonata movement with no score provided. There are two types of tasks in this exercise. First you must answer a series of questions similar to those above that will accompany each movement. The second task involves identifying formal sections and their keys. As you listen to the movement, numbers will be called out that represent points in the formal structure. You should answer the questions that correspond to these numbers.

Haydn, Symphony no. 45 in F#minor, "Farewell Symphony," Hob. I:45, *Allegro assai*

In mm. 1–16 (essentially one large phrase), the harmony changes every two measures except for a couple of spots: identify each harmony in the blanks provided.

mm.	1–2	3–4	5–6	7–8	9	10	11–12	13	14	15–16
	___	___	___	___	___	___	___	___	___	___

1. Name the formal segment. What key is it in?
2. Name the formal segment. What key does it begin in?
3. Name the formal segment. What key is it in? What is the origin of this material?
4. Name the formal segment. Has this been heard before and, if so, how does it differ from its earlier appearance?
5. Name the formal segment? What is unusual about it and why?
6. What type of transition occurs in the exposition? To what tonal area does it lead? A sequence appears in it; what type?
7. In what tonal area does the exposition close?
8. How long is the retransition?

CHAPTER 34

New Harmonic Tendencies

Exercises for: Plagal Relations, Reciprocal Process, Semitonal Voice Leading, and Ambiguity

ASSIGNMENT 34.1

ANALYSIS

DVD 1
CH 34
TRACK 1

EXERCISE 34.1

The excerpts below contain ambiguities resulting from modal mixture, semitonal voice leading, the reciprocal process, and enharmonic puns. Bracket the area or areas in which tonal ambiguity occurs. Label the type of ambiguity, and answer any accompanying questions.

A. Wagner, *Das Rheingold*, act I, scene 3 (Alberich demonstrates the magical powers of the Tarnhelm.)

In what key is this example? Is there a functional harmonic progression? Begin by looking at the excerpt's close.

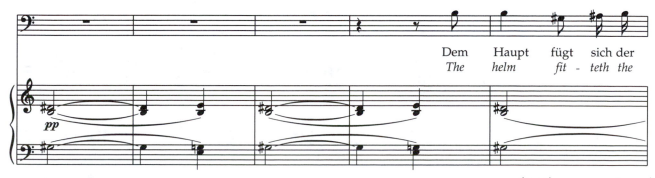

(continues on next page)

Helm: ob sich der Zau - ber auch zeigt?   Nacht   und Ne - bel
head: *now will the spell   al - so speed?*   *Night   and dark - ness*

B. Beethoven, Symphony no. 7 in A major, op. 92, *Vivace* and *Presto*.
    The first excerpt from Beethoven's Seventh Symphony begins on V/A. What key succeeds A major, and how is it secured? The second excerpt also illustrates a tonal motion. Compare and contrast the two methods of tonicization.

1. *Vivace:*

2. *Presto:*

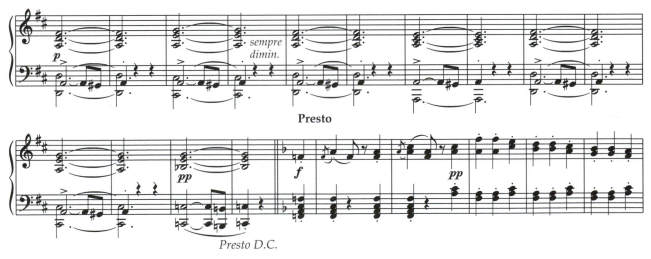

LISTENING

DVD 1
CH 34
TRACK 2

EXERCISE 34.2 Dictation

Notate bass and soprano voices, and provide a roman numeral analysis. Finally, in a few sentences describe the type of ambiguity involved.

WRITING

EXERCISE 34.3 Figured Bass

Fill in inner voices and include a second-level analysis.

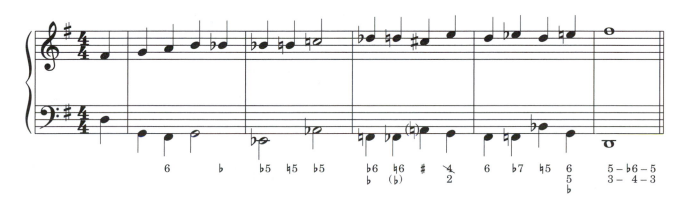

PLAYING

EXERCISE 34.4 Warmup and Review

Complete the tasks below.

A. Modulate from E major to ♭III by using modal mixture in the home key to prepare the new key. You may write out a basic sketch of what you will be playing. Analyze your work. Also include in your example:

1. A D2 (−5/+4) or A2 (−3/+4) sequence in either key. You may use either a diatonic or an applied chord sequence.
2. A tonicization of the Neapolitan.
3. An expansion of the pre-dominant area in ♭III that includes both the Ger⁶ and Ger⁷ chord.

B. Add inner voices to the unfigured bass and soprano melody below. Analyze and transpose to one other key of your choice.

ASSIGNMENT 34.2

ANALYSIS

DVD 1
CH 34
TRACK 3

EXERCISE 34.5

The excerpts below contain ambiguities resulting from modal mixture, semitonal voice leading, the reciprocal process, and enharmonic puns. Bracket the area or areas in which tonal ambiguity occurs. Label the type of ambiguity and answer any accompanying questions.

A. Brahms, "Mein Herz ist schwer" ("My Heart Is Heavy"), op. 94, no. 3

This song is in G minor; discuss the tonic's strength and function at the close.

B.   Bizet, *Carmen*, Chanson and Duet, act 1, no. 9

(continues on next page)

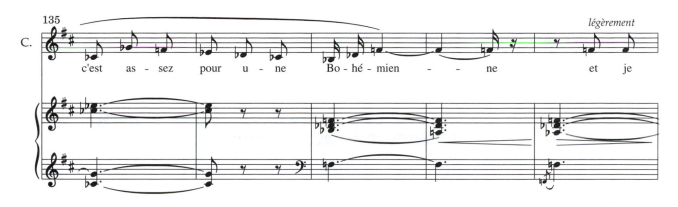

1. What key is established at mm. 97–98?
2. Name the harmonic device used at mm. 98–101.
3. Write in the score the roman numeral analysis for mm. 104–109 and 120–123.
4. Label the progression at m. 112–116.
5. What harmonic or voice-leading principle is used at mm. 123–128 and mm. 129–132?

LISTENING

DVD 1
CH 34
TRACK 4

EXERCISE 34.6 Dictation

Notate the bass voice, and provide a roman numeral analysis. Finally, in a few sentences describe the type of ambiguity involved.

A.   Brahms, "An die Nachtigall" ("To the Nightingale"), op. 46, no. 4

B. Beethoven, Symphony no. 2 in D major, op. 36, *Allegro molto*
Provide missing bass notes and add one more chord to the end to resolve the bass.

KEYBOARD

EXERCISE 34.7 Warmup and Review

Continue the progressions below based on the pivot chord instructions. Transpose to two other keys of your choice.

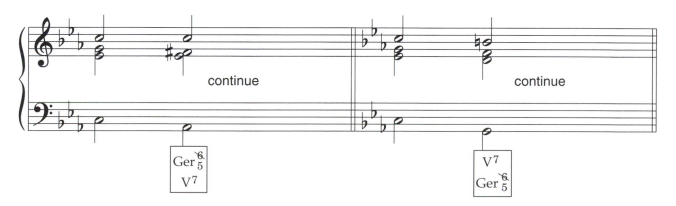

EXERCISE 34.8

Realize and analyze the figured bass in four-voice keyboard style.

Assignments for Enharmonic Usage of Diminished Seventh Chords and Off-Tonic Beginnings/Double Tonality

ASSIGNMENT 34.3

ANALYSIS

DVD 1
CH 34
TRACK 5

EXERCISE 34.9 Enharmonically Reinterpreted Diminished Seventh Chords

Mark the pivot in the examples below, which modulate by means of an enharmonically reinterpreted diminished seventh chord.

A.

B.

C. Wolf, "Verschling' der Abgrund meines liebsten hütte" ("May the Abyss Swallow Up My Beloved's Cottage"), *Italienisches Liederbuch*, no. 45

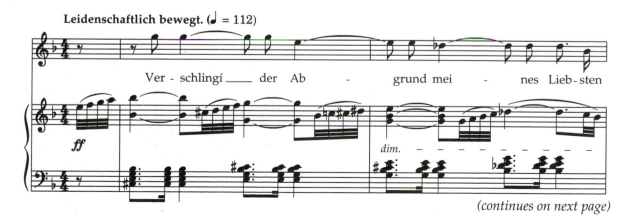

Leidenschaftlich bewegt. (♩ = 112)

Ver - schlingí____ der Ab - grund mei - nes Lieb - sten

ff

dim.

(continues on next page)

Hüt-te,

p ———————— *cresc.*

EXERCISE 34.10 Figured Bass

Realize the figured bass below in four voices. It includes at least one and perhaps more enharmonic modulations using the diminished seventh chord. Then, be able to sing either the bass or the soprano voice while playing the other three voices on the piano. Analyze.

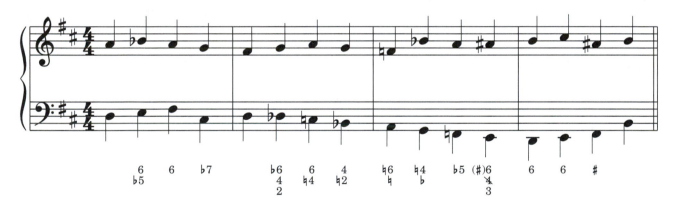

DVD 1
CH 34
TRACK 6

EXERCISE 34.11 Analysis/Dictation

Determine the goals of harmonic motion for the modulating passages below. Note values below the staff indicate harmonic rhythm. Then, notate the bass and soprano and provide roman numerals. Expect both diatonic and mixture pivots as well as enharmonic diminished sevenths. Use figured bass notation to label tones of figuration. Finally, add logical inner voices, focusing on enharmonic diminished sevenths.

A.

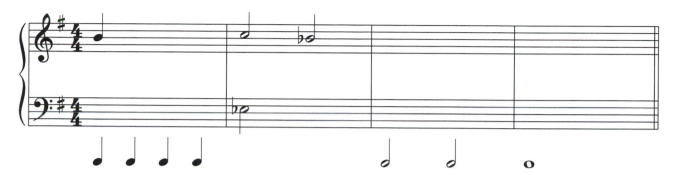

B.

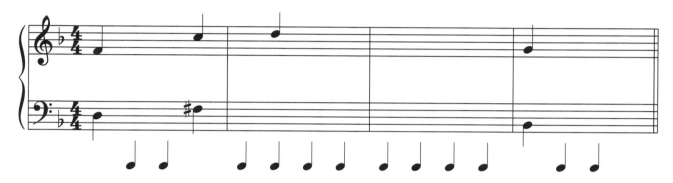

ASSIGNMENT 34.4

ANALYSIS

EXERCISE 34.12 Enharmonically Reinterpreted Diminished Seventh Chords

DVD 1
CH 34
TRACK 7

Mark the pivot in the examples below, which modulate by means of an enharmonically reinterpreted diminished seventh chord. Analyze the remaining chords with roman numerals.

A.

B.

LISTENING

DVD 1
CH 34
TRACK 8

EXERCISE 34.13 Analysis-Dictation

Determine the goals of harmonic motion for the modulating passages below, where note values below the staff indicate harmonic rhythm. Then notate the bass and soprano and provide roman numerals. Expect both diatonic and mixture pivots, as well as enharmonic diminished sevenths. Use figured bass notation to label tones of figuration. Finally, add logical inner voices, focusing on enharmonic diminished sevenths.

A.

B.

WRITING

EXERCISE 34.14 Figured Bass

Realize the figured bass below, which contains an enharmonic modulation that uses the diminished seventh chord. Analyze, including the pivot chord.

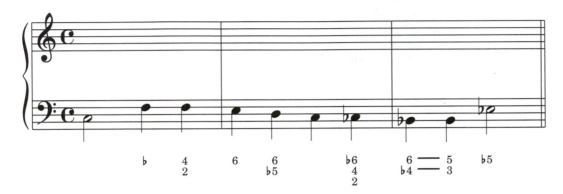

ASSIGNMENT 34.5

ANALYSIS

EXERCISE 34.15 Enharmonically Reinterpreted Diminished Seventh Chords

DVD 1
CH 34
TRACK 9

Mark the pivot in the examples below, which modulate by means of an enharmonically reinterpreted diminished seventh chord.

A. Wagner, Overture, *Der fliegende Holländer (The Flying Dutchman)*.

B.   Beethoven, Symphony no. 2 in D major, op. 36, *Larghetto*
      Begin by finding cadences, Then determine how the reinterpreted diminished seventh secures the key.

WRITING

EXERCISE 34.16 Figured Bass

Realize the figured bass below, which contains an enharmonic modulation that uses the diminished seventh chord. Analyze, including the pivot chord.

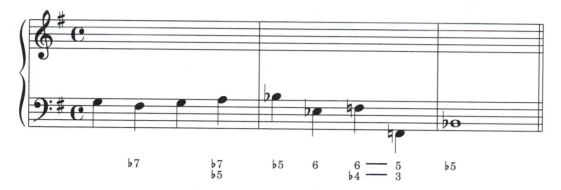

LISTENING

DVD 1
CH 34
TRACK 10

EXERCISE 34.17 Analysis/Dictation

Determine the goals of harmonic motion for the modulating passages below, where note values below the staff indicate harmonic rhythm. Then notate the bass and soprano and provide roman numerals. Expect both diatonic and mixture pivots as well as enharmonic diminished sevenths. Use figured bass notation to label tones of figuration. Finally, add logical inner voices, focusing on enharmonic diminished sevenths.

A.

B.

EXERCISE 34.18 Enharmonic Modulation by Means of Diminished Seventh Chords

A. Use the diminished seventh chord D–F–A♭–C♭ to modulate from E♭ major to C major

B. interpret each member of the diminished seventh chord C♯–E–G–B♭ as a root that leads to its own tonic. Be able to spell the chord correctly in each of the four keys. Then, play a progression that begins in one of the keys and includes the diminished seventh as a pivot that leads to one of the other distantly related keys.

ASSIGNMENT 34.6

WRITING

EXERCISE 34.19 Figured Bass

Realize the figured bass below, which contains an enharmonic modulation that uses the diminished seventh chord. Analyze, including the pivot chord.

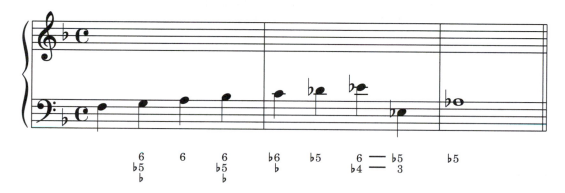

EXERCISE 34.20 Dictation

DVD 1
CH 34
TRACK 11

Notate bass and soprano in the progressions that modulate by enharmonic diminished sevenths. Analyze, marking the pivot carefully. Begin by determining the new key; then work backward from the cadence until you encounter the diminished seventh chord. Hint: A diminished seventh chord will often appear twice, first in its usual diatonic context, and then later in its enharmonic "chameleon-like" guise, to prepare the new key.

A.

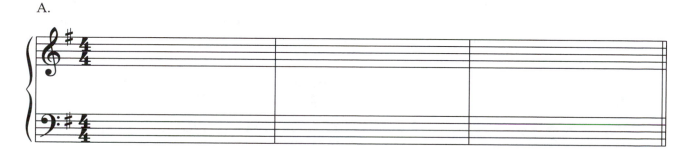

B.

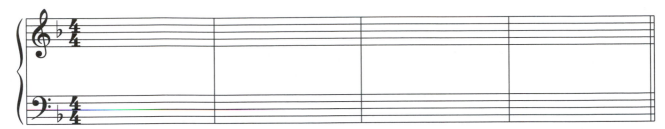

KEYBOARD

EXERCISE 34.21

Study the following examples that enharmonically reinterpret a diminished seventh chord to modulate to distant keys. Then, play the short progressions and specify the key to which the diminished seventh leads. Finally, play longer progressions (c. 6–8 chords) that establish the initial key, C major. Modulate by means of the diminished seventh chord and close with a strong cadence in the new key.

A.   B.   C.   D.

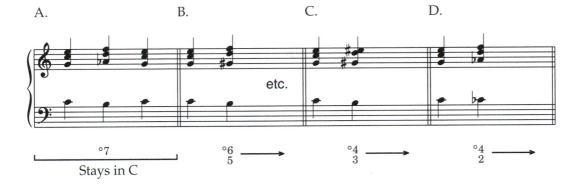

ANALYSIS

DVD 1
CH 34
TRACK 12

EXERCISE 34.22

Below are examples that do not begin on the tonic. Study each carefully, determining how best to interpret the off-tonic structure within the overall key scheme.

A. Lamm, "Saturday in the Park"

B. Schubert, Waltz, *12 Ländler*, op. 171, no. 4, D. 790

ASSIGNMENT 34.7

ANALYSIS

DVD 1
CH 34
TRACK 13

EXERCISE 34.23

Below are examples that do not begin on the tonic. Study each carefully, determining how best to interpret the off-tonic structure within the overall key scheme.

A. Schubert, Waltz, *18 German Dances and Ecossaises*, op. 33, no. 5, D. 783

B. Mendelssohn, "Wedding March," *Midsummer's Night Dream*, op. 61

LISTENING

DVD 1
CH 34
TRACK 14

EXERCISE 34.24 Dictation

Listen to and notate the outer voices of these examples, which modulate by means the three types of pivot chords we have discussed: diatonic, mixture, and enharmonic. Provide roman numerals and interpret the pivot chord. The possible tonal destinations in major are ii, ♭II, iii, IV, V, ♭VI, vi, VI; in minor, the possibilities are III, iv, v, and VI.

A.

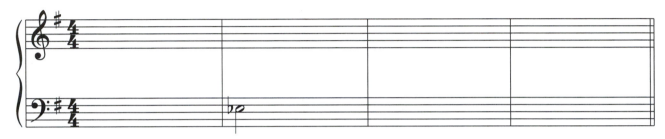

B.

C.

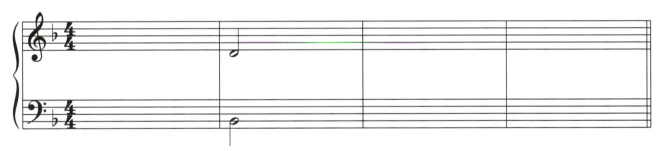

WRITING

EXERCISE 34.25 Composition

Using an enharmonically reinterpreted diminished-seventh chord, write a modulating consequent phrase to the given antecedent phrase. Note that the diminished-seventh chord is prepared in the antecedent phrase. Analyze, and play your solution.

Additional Exercises

LISTENING

DVD 1
CH 34
TRACK 15

EXERCISE 34.26 Dictation

Notate bass and soprano in the progression below, which modulates by means of enharmonic diminished sevenths. Analyze, marking the pivot carefully. Begin by determining the new key; then work backward from the cadence until you encounter the diminished seventh chord. Hint: A diminished seventh chord will often appear twice, first in its usual diatonic context, and then later in its enharmonic "chameleon-like" guise, to prepare the new key.

upbeat

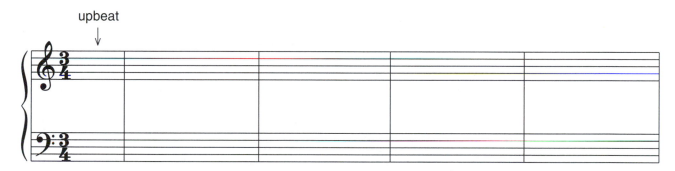

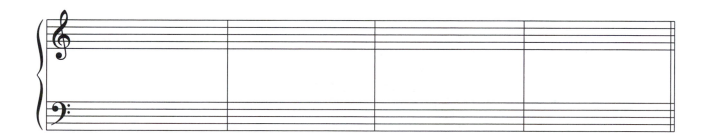

EXERCISE 34.27 Dictation

Listen to and notate the outer voices of these examples, which modulate by using the three types of pivot chords we have discussed: diatonic, mixture, and enharmonic. Provide roman numerals and interpret the pivot chord. The possible tonal destinations in major are ii, ♭II, iii, IV, V, ♭VI, vi, and VI; in minor, the possibilities are III, iv, v, and VI.

A.

B.

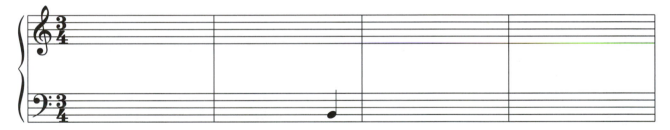

C.   begins on beat 3

WRITING

EXERCISE 34.28 Figured Bass

Construct a good soprano, then fill in the inner voices. Include a second-level
analysis that reflects the large-scale harmonic progression.

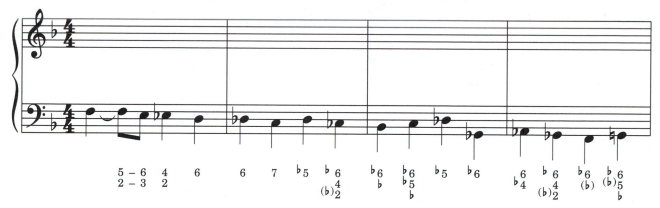

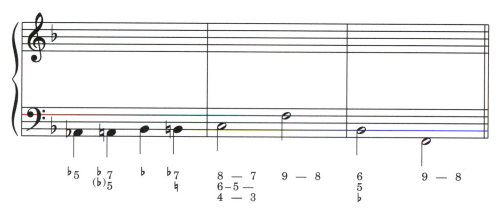

ANALYSIS

EXERCISE 34.29

Below are examples that do not begin on the tonic. Study each carefully, determining how best to interpret the off-tonic structure within the overall key scheme.

A. Wolf, "Nein, junger Herr" (No, Young Sir"), *Italienisches Liederbuch*, no. 12

(continues on next page)

Nein, jun - ger Herr, so treibt man's nicht, für wahr; man sorgt da -

C. Schubert, Waltz, *Letzte waltzer*, op. 127, no. 15, D. 146

COMPOSITION

EXERCISE 34.30

Sing or play the tune below to determine the harmonic rhythm, implied harmonies, cadences, and form. Then, harmonize it. Create an accompanimental pattern, then accompany a soloist who plays the given melody.

CHAPTER 35

The Rise of Symmetrical Harmony in Tonal Music

Exercises for Augmented Triad and Altered V7 Chords

ASSIGNMENT 35.1

ANALYSIS

DVD 1
CH 35
TRACK 1

EXERCISE 35.1

Analyze the examples below, which contain augmented triads and altered dominant seventh chords. Determine whether the dissonant pitches are tones of figuration (usually passing tones) or chordal members. Use figured bass notation. Passing tones are represented by a horizontal line (e.g., "5—#5"). Chromatic alterations of chord members are shown by placing the alterations before the arabic numbers.

For example

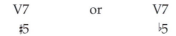

A.

B.

C.

LISTENING

EXERCISE 35.2 Analysis Dictation.

Listen to the following examples and study the given upper voices. Then notate the bass and provide a roman numeral analysis.

A.

B.

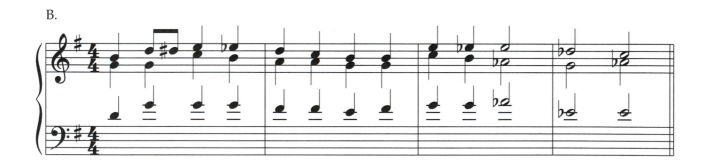

C.

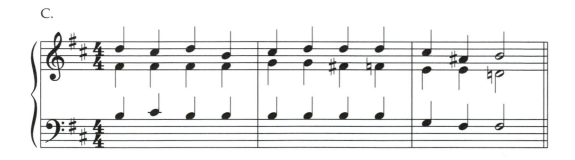

KEYBOARD

EXERCISE 35.3 Semitonal voice leading

Below are the outer voices of four implied dominant seventh chords whose roots are minor thirds apart. Determine the roots for each chord, then add the missing chordal members in the inner voices. Notice how each chord connects to the next by common tone or half step motion. Transpose the four-chord pattern down a whole step and up a whole step. Extra credit: Sing one of the outer voices while playing the other three.

WRITING

EXERCISE 35.4 Altered Triads and Seventh Chords

Complete these tasks in four voices.

A.   B.

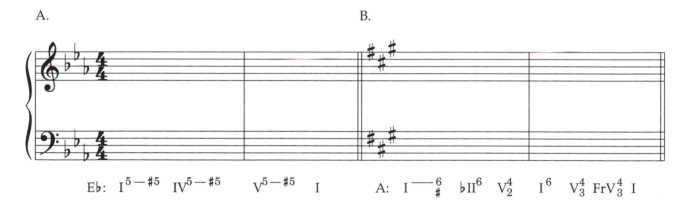

Eb: $I^{5-\sharp5}$ $IV^{5-\sharp5}$ $V^{5-\sharp5}$ I A: $I^{6}_{\sharp}$ $\flat II^6$ V^4_2 I^6 V^4_3 FrV^4_3 I

ASSIGNMENT 35.2

ANALYSIS

DVD 1
CH 35
TRACK 3

EXERCISE 35.5

Analyze the examples below, which contain augmented triads and altered dominant-seventh chords. Determine whether the dissonant pitches are tones of figuration (usually passing tones) or chordal members. Use figured bass notation. Passing tones are represented by a horizontal line (e.g., "5—#5"). Chromatic alterations of chord members are shown by placing the alterations before the arabic numbers.

For example:

V7	or	V7
#5		♭5

A. Schumann, "Fabel" ("Fable"), *Phantasiestücke*, op, 12, no. 6.

Be aware that this excerpt does not begin in the tonic.

B. Beethoven, Variation XIV, *Diabelli* Variations, Op. 120.

Suspensions create the dissonant harmony that appears on the downbeat of m. 3.

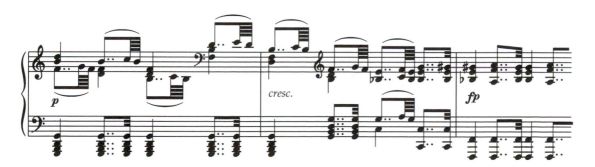

C. Puccini, *Madama Butterfly*, act I.

What sequence does Puccini use?

LISTENING

DVD 1
CH 35
TRACK 4

EXERCISE 35.6 Analysis/Dictation

Below are the upper parts of examples. Listen to and study what is given, then notate the bass and provide a roman numeral analysis.

A.   Beethoven, Bagatelle in G minor, op. 119, no. 1

B.   Haydn, String Quartet in G minor, op. 74, no. 2, Hob. III:74, *Andante grazioso*

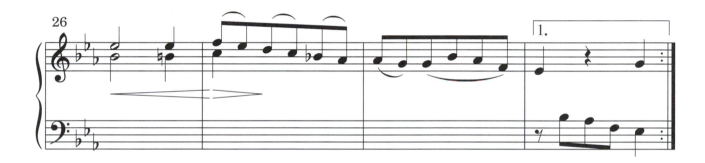

C.   Schumann, *Scherzo, Klavierstücke*, op. 32.

Be aware that there is an enharmonic modulation.

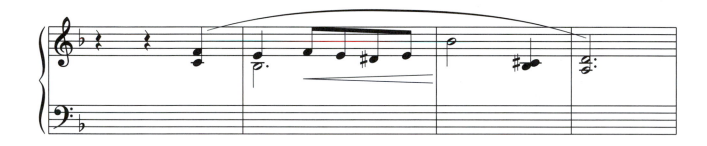

Assignments for CT°7 and CT ⁺6

ASSIGNMENT 35.3

ANALYSIS

DVD 1
CH 35
TRACK 5

EXERCISE 35.7 Chromatic Common-Tone Harmonies

Be aware that diminished sevenths and augmented sixths may be used either as common-tone chords (in which they contrapuntally prolong an underlying harmony) or as functional chords (in which they participate in the harmonic progression (augmented sixths function as pre-dominants, and diminished sevenths function as dominants). Employ a two-level analysis, making sure that you distinguish between contrapuntal and harmonic functions.

A.

B.

C.

WRITING

EXERCISE 35.8 Writing Common-Tone Harmonies

Use common-tone diminished sevenths to embellish tonic and dominant.

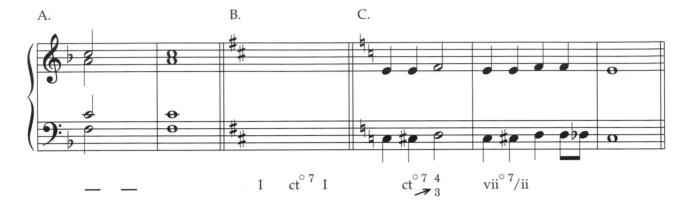

LISTENING

DVD 1
CH 35
TRACK 6

EXERCISE 35.9 Variations and Expansion of Harmonic Model

You will hear a model, which is followed by a series of variations, or expansions, on the model. On a separate piece of manuscript paper notate the outer voices and provide a roman numeral analysis.

Model A

Expansion 1

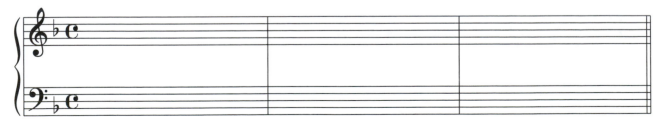

Expansion 2

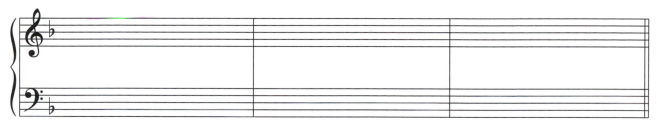

Expansion 3

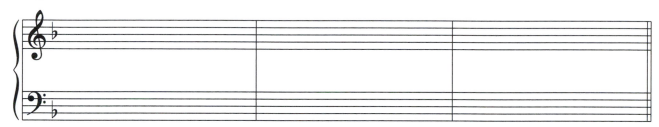

Expansion 4

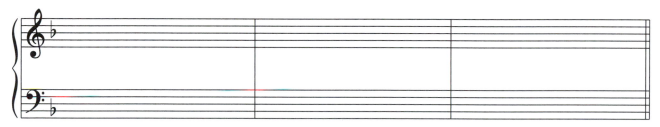

LISTENING

DVD 1
CH 35
TRACK 8

EXERCISE 35.12 Analysis/Dictation.

Notate the missing soprano and bass voice for the excerpts below, which illustrate common-tone harmonies. Add logical inner voices.

A.   B.

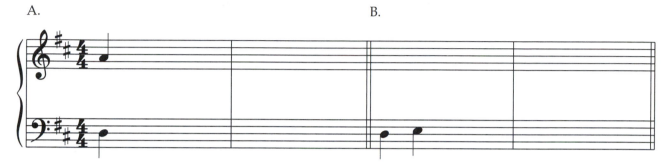

C.   Beethoven, Variation XII, *Diabelli* Variations, Op. 120

ASSIGNMENT 35.5

LISTENING:

DVD 1
CH 35
TRACK 9

EXERCISE 35.13 Analysis/Dictation

Notate the missing soprano and bass voice for the excerpts below that illustrate augmented triads, altered dominant seventh chords, and common-tone chords (diminished sevenths and augmented sixths). Add logical inner voices.

A.

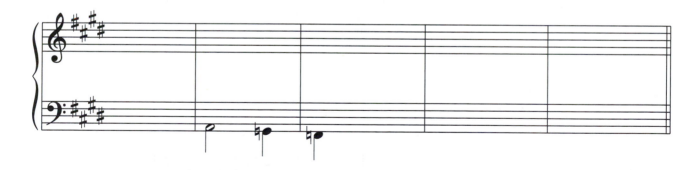

B.

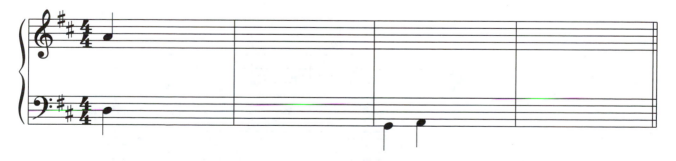

WRITING

EXERCISE 35.14 Figured Bass

Realize the figured bass below in four voices. Analyze.

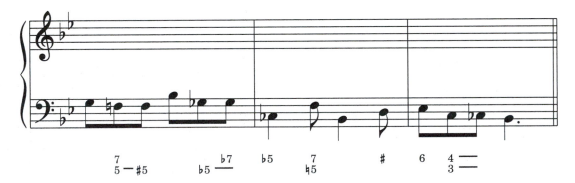

EXERCISE 35.15 Melody Harmonization

Set each soprano fragment in four voices, including at least three chromatic chords in each example. You may use modal mixture, applied chords, common-tone harmonies, altered dominant and dominant seventh chords, ♭II chords, and augmented sixth chords. Analyze.

A.

b:

B.

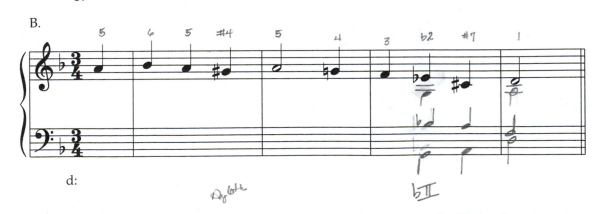

d:

ASSIGNMENT 35.6

LISTENING

EXERCISE 35.16 Variations and Expansion of Harmonic Models

The model below is followed by six variations, or expansions. Notate the outer voices and provide a roman numeral analysis.

Model A

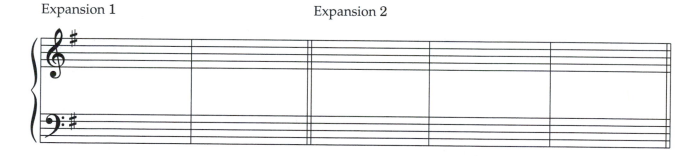

Expansion 1   Expansion 2

Expansion 3   Expansion 4

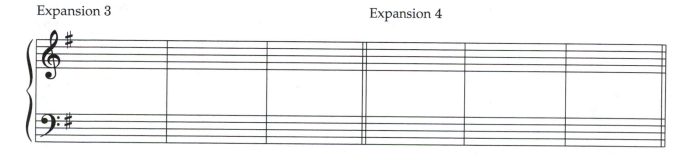

(continues on next page)

Expansion 5

Expansion 6

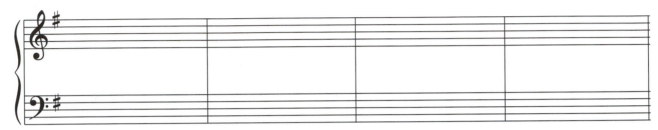

WRITING

EXERCISE 35.17 Unfigured Bass

Add inner voices to create a four-voice texture. Use ct°7s where possible. Analyze.

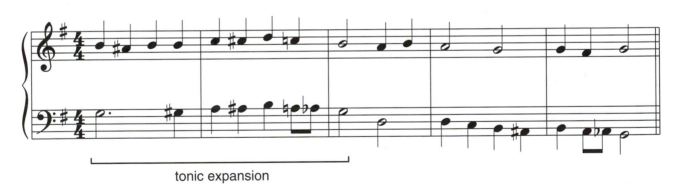

tonic expansion

EXERCISE 35.18 Melody Harmonization

Set the soprano line in four voices. Include at least four chromatic chords. You may use modal mixture, applied chords, common-tone harmonies, altered dominant and dominant seventh chords, ♭II chords, and augmented sixth chords. Analyze.

d:

Additional Exercises

EXERCISE 35.19 Melody Harmonization

Set each soprano fragment in four voices, including at least three chromatic chords in Exercise A. You may use modal mixture, applied chords, common-tone harmonies, altered dominant and dominant seventh chords, ♭II chords, and augmented sixth chords. Analyze. For Exercise B, include one of each of the following (but not necessarily in this order): altered dominant, applied dominant, Fr V $\frac{4}{3}$, and common-tone diminished seventh chord. Analyze.

A.

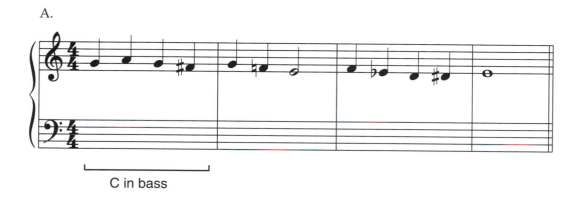

C in bass

B.

EXERCISE 35.20 Figured Basses

Realize the figured basses below in four voices. Analyze.

A.

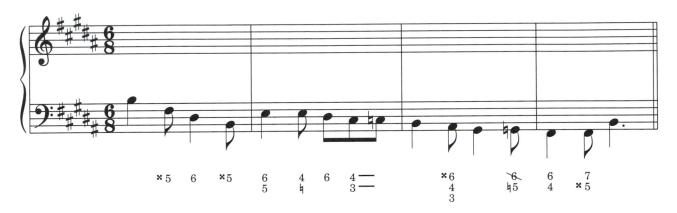

B.

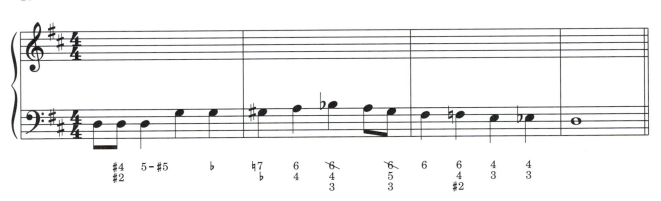

CHAPTER 36

Melodic and Harmonic Symmetry Combine: Chromatic Sequences

Assignments for Chromatic Sequences

ASSIGNMENT 36.1

ANALYSIS

DVD 1
CH 36
TRACK 1

EXERCISE 36.1 Analysis of Chromatic Sequences

Bracket and label each sequence in the following exercises. Circle each bass note involved in the sequence. Do not analyze each harmony within the sequence—only the harmonies that begin and end the sequence. Then determine the underlying tonal progression.

A. Carissimi, "Et ululantes filii Ammon" ("And Weeping, the Children of Ammon") from *Jephthah*

B.   Schubert, Symphony no. 4 in C minor, "Tragic," D. 417, *Adagio molto—Allegro vivace*

C.   Schumann, Symphony no. 1 in B♭ major, "Spring," op. 38, *Andante un poco maestoso—Allegro molto vivace*

WRITING

EXERCISE 36.2 Pattern Completion

1. Study the following sequential models, then write three copies.
2. End with a strong cadence. Label each sequence type.
3. Transpose each sequence to another key of your choice.
4. Begin by writing the first of two-chord patterns, which must be consonant (major or minor) triads. Then add the helping (second) chord to each repetition.

A.

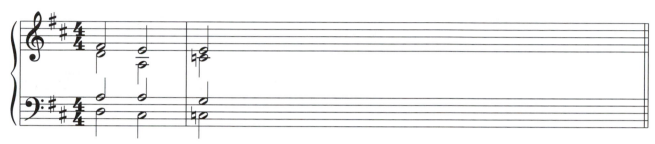

B.   Three voices only

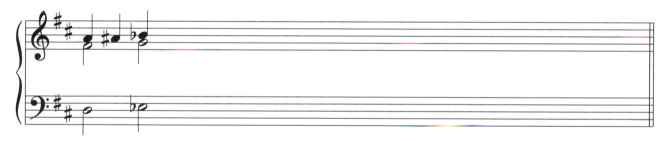

C.   The model begins on beat 3

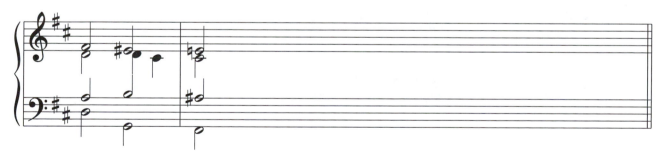

D.

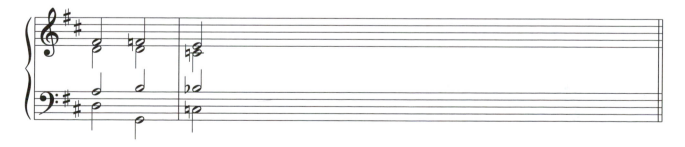

LISTENING

EXERCISE 36.3 Analysis/Dictation of Diatonic and Chromatic Sequences

DVD 1
CH 36
TRACK 2

Label the sequence type, bracket begin and ending points of the sequence on the incomplete score, then notate the bass line.

A.

B.

ASSIGNMENT 36.2

ANALYSIS

DVD 1
CH 36
TRACK 3

EXERCISE 36.4

Bracket and label each sequence in the following exercises. Circle each bass note involved in the sequence. Analyze only the harmonies that begin and end the sequence and then determine the underlying tonal progression.

A.   Mendelssohn, Prelude in B minor, op. 104, no. 2

B.   Beethoven, *Menuetto*, Symphony no. 1 in C major, op. 21

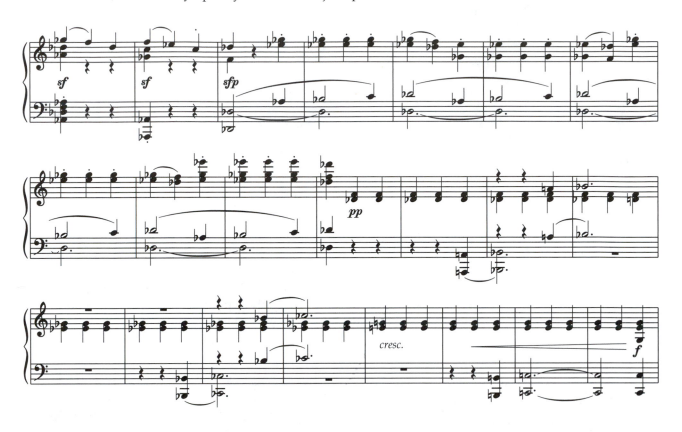

C.   Donizetti, "Esci fuggi" from *Lucia di Lammermoor*, act II, scene 5

(continues on next page)

tà, sì, - quan - te vol - tead un so - lo tor - men - to
thral, ah, heav'n - ly love hath a balm for thy sor - row,

drà, sì, sì, la mac - chia d'ol - trag - gio sì ne - ro
fall, the maid - en's heart hath by thee - been per - vert - ed

drà, sì, sì, la mac - chia d'ol - trag - gio sì ne - ro, __ col tuo
fall, the maid - en's heart hath by thee been per - vert - ed, __ We have

Più allegro

LISTENING

**DVD 1
CH 36
TRACK 4**

EXERCISE 36.5 Analysis/Dictation of Diatonic and Chromatic Sequences

Label the sequence type; bracket begin and ending points of the sequence on the incomplete score; then notate the bass line.

A.

B.

(continues on next page)

WRITING

EXERCISE 36.6 Unfigured and Figured Basses

Complete the unfigured bass exercise (A) in *three* voices and include 7–6 suspensions. Complete the two figured bass exercises (B and C) in *four* voices. Label any sequences. Be aware of modulations.

A.

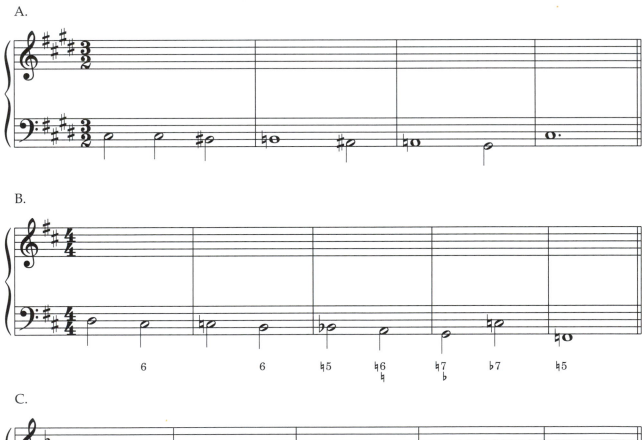

B.

C.

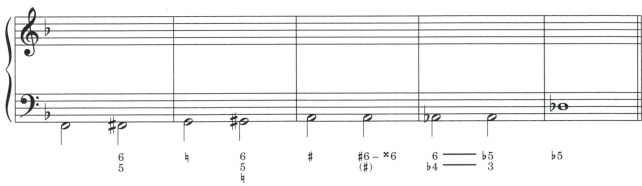

ASSIGNMENT 36.3

ANALYSIS

DVD 1
CH 36
TRACK 5

EXERCISE 36.7

These excerpts from Chopin and Beethoven contain multiple sequences. Circle and label each.

A.   Chopin, Piano Sonata in C minor, op. 4, BI 23, *Allegro maestoso*

(continues on next page)

B.   Beethoven, Piano Concerto no. 1 in C major, op. 15, *Allegro*

LISTENING

EXERCISE 36.8 Analysis/Dictation of Diatonic and Chromatic Sequences

Label the sequence type; bracket begin and ending points of the sequence on the incomplete score; then notate the bass line.

A. Beethoven, Piano Sonata no. 12 in A♭ major, op. 26, *Scherzo*

B. Beethoven, Symphony no. 3 in E♭ major, "Eroica," op. 55, *Allegro con brio*

WRITING

EXERCISE 36.9 Composition

Write two consequents to the given antecedent to create a parallel interrupted period and a contrasting progressive period. Label each period and analyze the harmonies.

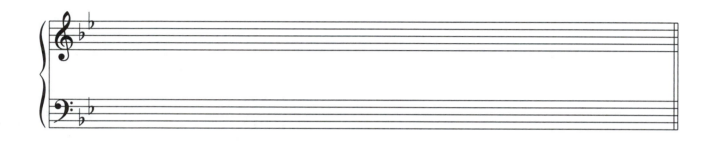

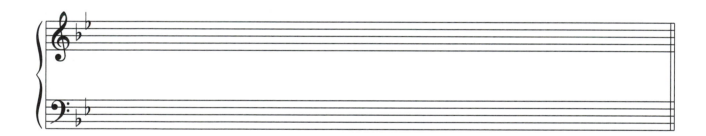

ASSIGNMENT 36.4

DVD 1
CH 36
TRACK 7

EXERCISE 36.10 Dictation of Sequences

Identify the sequence type and notate the bass voice.

A.

B.

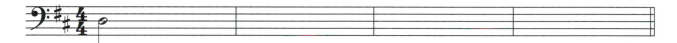

C.

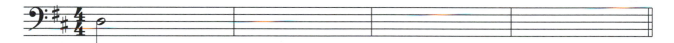

D.

WRITING

EXERCISE 36.11 Extended Illustrations

Complete any two of the following tasks.

A. Write a three-voice progression in F♯ minor that begins on tonic, moves through a sequence of descending six-three chords with 7–6 suspensions and chromatic bass, and leads to a cadential six-four chord. The dominant will move deceptively to a mixture chord, followed by a cadence in a chromatic, third-related key.

B. Write a three-voice progression in E♭ major that begins with an A2 (–3/ +4) sequence using applied V^6 chords that resolve to major triads. This sequence will move from I to III. Once you have arrived on III, treat it as a temporary tonic. Expand and cadence on III.

C. Write a three-voice progression in E♭ major that begins with a chromatic A2 (−3/+4) sequence, this time employing augmented triads that will serve as applied chords to the next chromatic chords. Move from I to III (e.g., I . . ♭II . . . ♮II . . .). Don't modulate to III, but find a convenient way to get back to tonic and cadence there.

D. Write a four-voice progression in G major that initially moves from I to iv via a chromatic D2 (−4/+3) sequence. Expand this pre-dominant with a voice exchange that includes an augmented sixth chord. Close with a PAC.

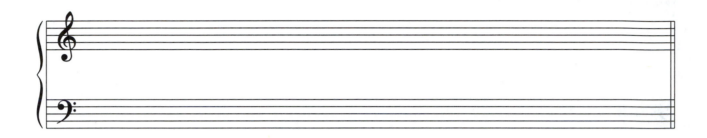

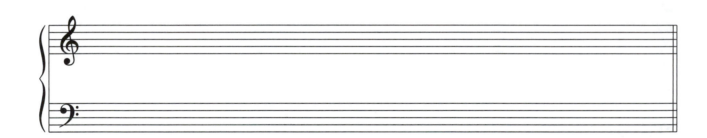

Assignments for Chromatic Sequences and Chromatic Contrary Motion Progressions

ASSIGNMENT 36.5

LISTENING

DVD 1
CH 36
TRACK 8

EXERCISE 36.12 Dictation of Sequences

Identify the sequence type and notate the bass voice.

A.

B.   Mendelssohn, Symphony no. 3 in A minor, "Scottish," op. 56, *Allegro, un poco agitato*

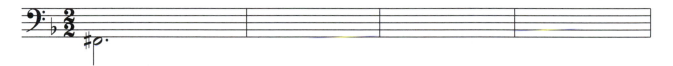

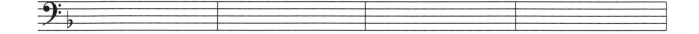

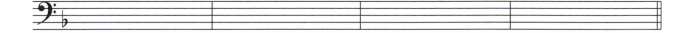

C.   Schumann, Symphony no. 2 in C major, op. 61, (in two) *Allegro*

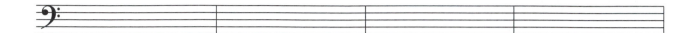

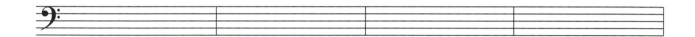

ANALYSIS

DVD 1
CH 36
TRACK 9

EXERCISE 36.13 Analysis of Chromatic Sequences and Contrary-Motion Chromaticism

Label and bracket any sequences in the examples below and analyze any harmonies outside of the sequence.

A.   Brahms, "Salome," op. 69, no. 8

Develop the idea that the chromaticism in this example might have been motivated by the text.

(continues on next page)

fraun   im ____ Land,   von   dem Berg ____ und ____ ü - ber ____ See! ____
from   the   Country, from the mountains and   across   the   Sea!

B.   Schubert, Violin Sonata in D major, D. 384, *Allegro*

WRITING

EXERCISE 36.14

Realize the figured basses below. The first example includes a complete soprano, but the second example presents an incomplete soprano line. Analyze.

A.

B.

KEYBOARD

EXERCISE 36.15

Continue the following sequence using chromatic voice exchange (to the key of A♭).

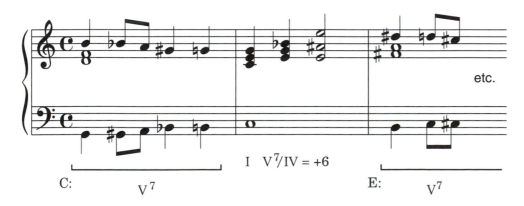

ASSIGNMENT 36.6

ANALYSIS

EXERCISE 36.16 Analysis of Chromatic Sequences and Contrary-Motion Chromaticism

Label and bracket sequences in the examples below and analyze harmonies outside the sequence.

A.   Schubert, String Quartet in G major, D. 887, *Allegro molto moderato*

(continues on next page)

B.   Schubert, "*Sanctus*," Mass no. 6 in E♭ major, D. 950

DVD 1
CH 36
TRACK 11

EXERCISE 36.17 Dictation

The contrary-motion chromatic progressions prolong either the tonic, dominant or the pre-dominant function. Notate outer voices, provide roman numerals, and bracket and label the expanded harmonic function.

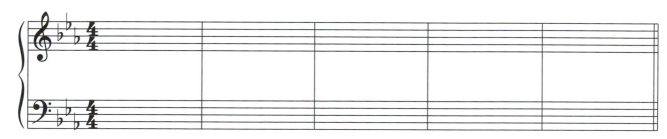

A.

B.

C.

EXERCISE 36.18 Figured Bass

Realize the figured bass below. Analyze.

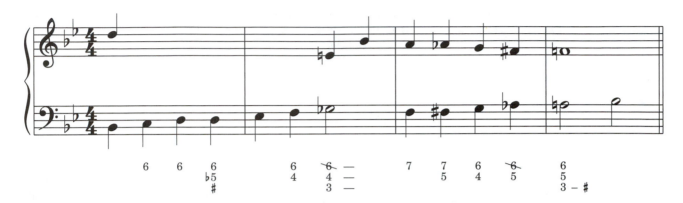

ASSIGNMENT 36.7

KEYBOARD

EXERCISE 36.19

Realize the following soprano and figured bass in keyboard style. Analyze. Be able to sing either outer voice while playing the remaining three.

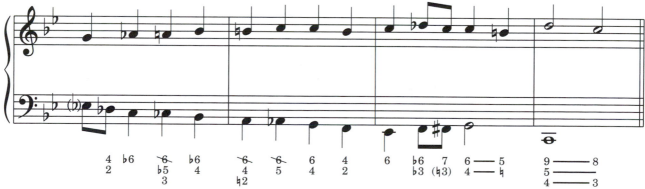

LISTENING

DVD 1
CH 36
TRACK 12

EXERCISE 36.20 Expansion and Variation of Model Progressions

Study the harmonic models below. Each is followed by a series of expansions and/or variations. On a separate sheet of manuscript paper, notate outer voices and provide roman numerals. Expect chromatic sequences and modulations.

Model #A:

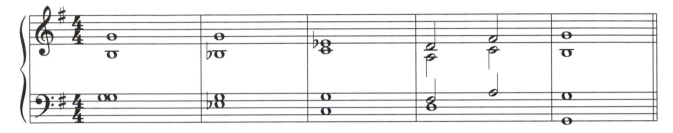

Model #B:

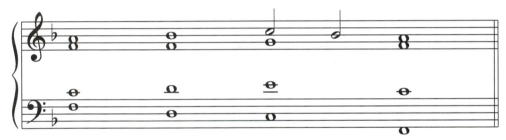

Model #C:

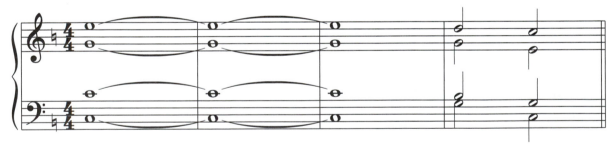

WRITING

EXERCISE 36.21 Soprano Harmonization

Harmonize in four voices the following soprano melodies; include each of the required elements. Analyze.

A.

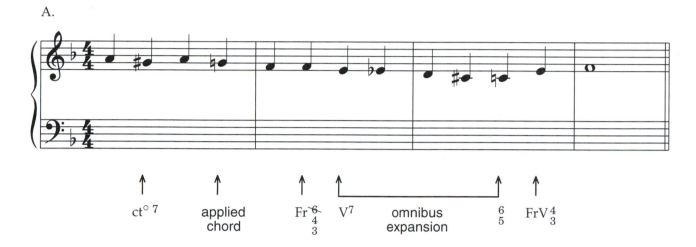

B.

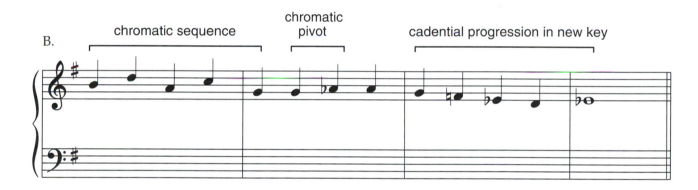

C.

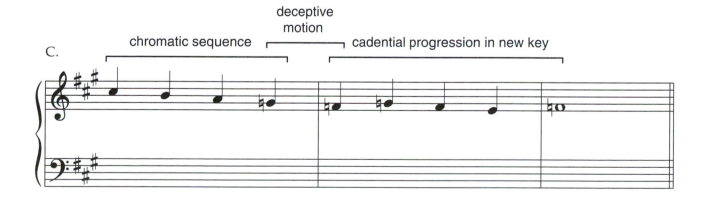

CHAPTER 37

At Tonality's Edge

Assignments for Sequential and Nonsequential Progressions

ASSIGNMENT 37.1

ANALYSIS

DVD 1
CH 37
TRACK 1

EXERCISE 37.1 Analysis of Progressions that Divide the Octave Evenly

Use second-level analytical brackets and specify whether each of the following excerpts illustrates an example of a sequential or nonsequential progression that divides the octave equally (into either major or minor thirds, each step of which is tonicized).

A. Wolf, "Und steht Ihr früh am Morgen auf" ("And When You Rise Early"), *Italienisches Liederbuch*, no. 34

(continues on next page)

B.

WRITING

EXERCISE 37.2 Figured Bass

Realize the figured bass below in four voices. Include a roman-numeral analysis. Mark all sequences and tonicizations.

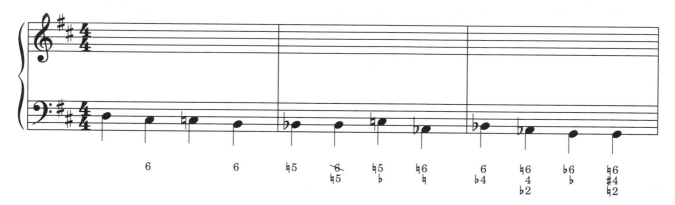

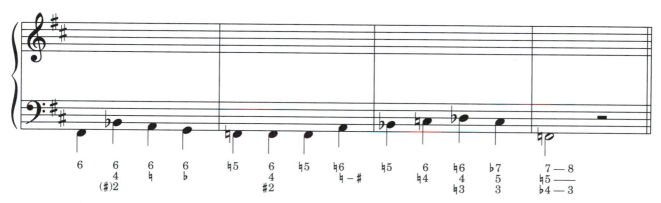

LISTENING

EXERCISE 37.3 Analysis/Dictation: Potpourri of Various Types of Tonicization.

The examples below tonicize or modulate to diatonic or chromatic keys. Add missing bass pitches. Analyze. Modulatory techniques include the following:

1. pivot chord (diatonic, mixture chord, or enharmonic (diminished seventh or German sixth))
2. sequence (diatonic or chromatic)
3. sequential progression

A.

B.

ASSIGNMENT 37.2

ANALYSIS

EXERCISE 37.4 Tchaikovsky, *Scherzo*, Symphony no. 4 in F minor, op. 36, *Pizzicato ostinato*

Below are several thematic and tonal areas as well as transitions that link formal sections of this famous movement. Determine the means by which each new tonal area is secured. Then, interpret the large-scale tonal structure of the movement based on the unfolding keys. Summarize the results of your analysis in a few sentences.

(continues on next page)

WRITING

EXERCISE 37.5 Unfigured Bass

Consider the harmonic implications of the two-voice counterpoint below. Then, analyze and add the inner voices to create an SATB texture.

ASSIGNMENT 37.3

LISTENING

EXERCISE 37.6   Analysis/Dictation: Potpourri of Various Types of Tonicization

The examples below tonicize or modulate to diatonic or chromatic keys. Add missing bass pitches. Analyze. Modulatory techniques include the following:

1. pivot chord (diatonic, mixture chord, or enharmonic (diminished seventh or German sixth)
2. sequence (diatonic or chromatic)
3. sequential progression

A.

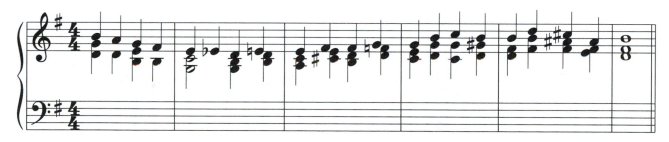

B.

WRITING

EXERCISE 37.7 Figured Bass

Realize the figured bass below in four voices. Analyze and summarize in a sentence or two any large-scale tonal patterns.

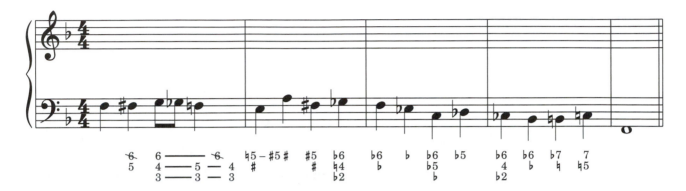

KEYBOARD

EXERCISE 37.8 Driving the Omnibus

Play progression A in keyboard style as written, and then transpose to the key of F major (you'll be starting on C_7 since this omnibus expands the dominant). Then, try leaving the sequence at various points, treating the first chord of any measure as a V_7 (see Example B) or as a Ger 6 (see Example C).

A.

B.

C.

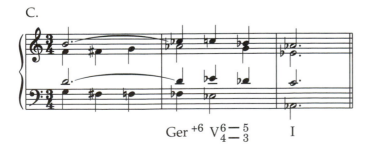

ASSIGNMENT 37.4

LISTENING

DVD 1
CH 37
TRACK 3

EXERCISE 37.9 Analysis/Dictation

You will hear two excerpts from Alexander Scriabin's piano preludes. Notate the bass and provide a roman numeral and second-level analysis.

A. Scriabin, Prelude in Ab major, op. 11, no. 17

B. Scriabin, Prelude in C major, op. 35, no. 3

ANALYSIS

EXERCISE 37.10

Chopin, Mazurka in B major, op. 56, no. 1, BI 153
You are given the opening passages for each of the large sections in Chopin's
Mazurka. What is the probable form? Focus on tricky harmonic areas, such as the
sequential passage that opens the piece and the transitional and retransitional passages that link larger sections. In a few sentences, discuss what appears to be the
large-scale tonal structure of the entire piece.

DVD 1
CH 37
TRACK 4

A3

ASSIGNMENT 37.5

ANALYSIS

EXERCISE 37.11

Below are examples from four of Wagner's operas, *Der fliegende Holländer (The Flying Dutchman)*, *Parsifal*, *Tristan und Isolde*, and *Die Walküre*. Analyze each excerpt, then compare and contrast the final three.

A.   Prelude to *Der fliegende Holländer (The Flying Dutchman)*

B.   "Zum letzten Liebesmahle" ("At the Last Meal of Love"), from *Parsifal*, act I

(continues on next page)

C. "Mild und leise" ("Mildly and Gently") (opening of "Liebestod") *Tristan und Isolde*, act III, scene 3

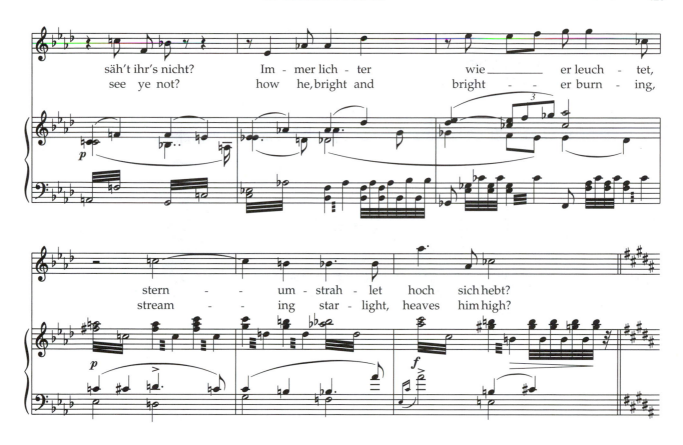

D. "Leb' wohl" ("Farewell") "Woton's Farewell" from *Die Walküre*, act 3, scene 3

KEYBOARD

EXERCISE 37.12 Brain Twister

Use the following sonorities (or their enharmonic equivalents) in at least two (2) different ways. (Hint: recall that enharmonic changes permit different harmonic destinations.)

A. C♯–E–G–B♭

B. E♭–G–B♭–D♭

C. C–D–F♯–A♭

LISTENING

DVD 1
CH 37
TRACK 5

EXERCISE 37.13

Notate the outer voices for the following chromatic modulations. Analyze.

A.

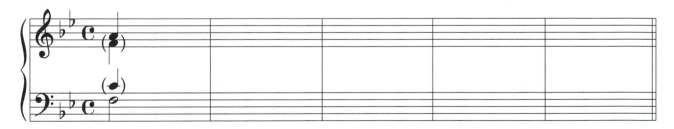

B.

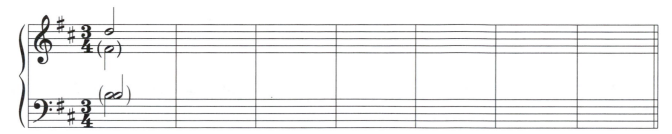

C.

D.

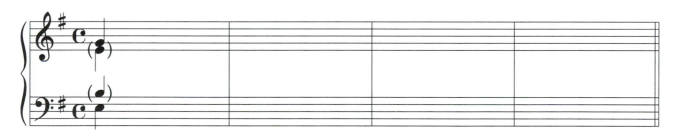

E.

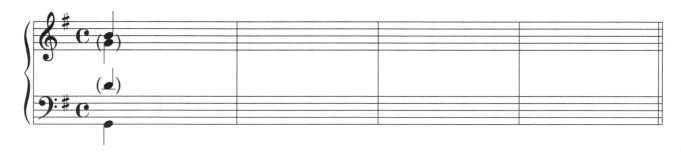

ASSIGNMENT 37.6

ANALYSIS

EXERCISE 37.14 Intervallic Cells

Trace repetitions of the circled intervallic cell labeling the transformation of each as follows: T (transposition), I (inversion), R (retrograde), RI (retrograde inversion), A (augmentation), and D (diminution). Repetitions may not be strict; for example, intervallic size between each pair of members of the cell may not be exact.

(continues on next page)

Additional Exercises

ANALYSIS

EXERCISE 37.15 Berg, "Nacht" ("Night"), from *Sieben frühe Lieder (Seven Early Songs)*, no. 1

DVD 1
CH 37
TRACK 6

This is the first song in a collection of songs written just as Berg's compositional voice was beginning to emerge. While composed in the shadow of the nineteenth century, these songs also look to the future. We will focus only on the song's opening measures, in which an ambiguous structure gradually gives way to a more traditional harmonic progression, a vivid juxtaposition of old and new styles. Consider the following issues in your analysis.

1. Recall that structure—and with it, clarity—is often postponed until the end of musical units.
2. Is the key signature unnecessary, or is Berg using it traditionally? If Berg incorporates it traditionally, you may be able to make some harmonic sense out of the opening of the song.
3. The opening of the song is reminiscent of the Scriabin prelude (op. 39, no. 2) that was discussed in the text. However, in this song the sonorities owe an even greater debt to the whole-tone scale. Recall from our earlier studies that the whole-tone scale comprises intervals whose number of half steps is evenly divided by 2. For example, a major second (2 half steps), major third (4), tritone (6), minor sixth (8), and minor seventh (10).
4. Notice how the song begins with a single pitch, E, to which is added an F♯. Is there some additive process that generates subsequent sonorities?
5. Study the translation of the text. Is Berg sensitive to its sentiments? If so, how?

Dämmern Wolken über Nacht und Tal,	Over night and valley the clouds grow dark,
Nebel schweben, Wasser rauschen sacht.	Mists are hovering, water rushes by.
Nun entschleiert sich's mit einemmal:	Now the covering veil is lifted:
O gib Acht! Gib Acht!	Come look! Look!
Weites . . .	Distant . . .